The Sufilive Series

The Sufilive Series
Volume 3

Spiritual Discourses of
Sultan al-Awliya
Mawlana Shaykh Muhammad
Nazim Adil al-Haqqani

PUBLISHED BY
INSTITUTE FOR SPIRITUAL AND CULTURAL ADVANCEMENT

Published and Distributed by:

Institute for Spiritual and Cultural Advancement (ISCA)
17195 Silver Parkway, #401
Fenton, MI 48430 USA
Tel: (888) 278-6624
Fax: (810) 815-0518
Email: staff@naqshbandi.org
Web: http://www.naqshbandi.org

First Edition: JULY 2010
THE SUFILIVE SERIES, Volume 3
ISBN 978-1-930409-77-4

Library of Congress Cataloging-in-Publication Data

Naqshbandi, Muhammad Nazim Adil al-Haqqani, 1922-
The Sufilive Series / Muhammad Nazim Adil al-Haqqani.
p. cm.
Includes bibliographical references.
ISBN 978-1-930409-77-4 (alk. paper)
1. Naqshabandiyah. 2. Islam--Doctrines. 3. Islam--Customs and practices. 4. Sufism. I. Title.
BP189.7.N352N365 2010
297.4'8--dc22
2010021437

PRINTED IN THE UNITED STATES OF AMERICA
15 14 13 12 11 05 06 07 08 09

Sultan al-Awliya, Mawlana Shaykh Muhammad Nazim Adil al-Haqqani (left), head of the Most Distinguished Naqshbandi-Haqqani Sufi Order, with Shaykh Hisham Kabbani. The daily live broadcast on Sufilive.com attracts thousands of viewers from around the world and all walks of life. Photo taken after the live broadcast. July 2010, Lefke, Cyprus.

Table of Contents

About the Author

Shaykh Muḥammad Nazim Adil was born in 1922 in Cyprus, into an aristocratic family deeply rooted in Ottoman culture. He and his siblings pursued higher education in Istanbul, and he received a degree in chemistry, a passion that later disinterested him when he could not save an ailing older brother from dying. Thereafter, he became deeply immersed in the study of traditional Islam and *tasāwwuf,* Sufism. Eventually he was led to the guide he had beheld in dreams.

In 1945, young Nazim became a disciple of Sulṭān al-Awlīyā, Shaykh ʿAbdAllāh al-Faʿiz ad-Daghestani of Damascus (d. 1973), 39th Master of the esteemed Naqshbandi-Haqqani Golden Chain that originates with Prophet Muḥammad, may the peace and blessing of God be upon him. In 1952, Grandshaykh ʿAbdAllāh married the young shaykh, Nazim, to another disciple who was like a daughter, Amina. Years before, her faithful family fled religious persecution in Communist Russia and settled in Turkey and later in Damascus. Shaykh Nazim and Hajjah Amina began married life near Grandshaykh ʿAbdAllāh's place on Jabal Qasiyoun, a famous area of Damascus, and later raised their growing family between Damascus and Cyprus.

Shaykh Nazim was often ordered by Grandshaykh ʿAbdAllāh into seclusion (*khalwah*), where he trained in advanced Sufi sciences and became disciplined in the ways of self-denial. During these times he was absent from home six months, a year, or longer. For more than twenty years he was responsible for large annual groups of pilgrims, and was also known for his grassroots walking tour of the Turkish countryside, from village to village, where he encouraged common folk to shun secular life and return to their Islamic heritage. He courageously defied a Turkish edict that outlawed public *adhān* (call to prayer) in its native Arabic, which led to its repeal.

In 1973, before Grandshaykh ʿAbdAllāh passed away, he appointed Mawlana Shaykh Nazim as his spiritual heir and successor. Shaykh Nazim then assumed the title Sulṭān al-Awlīyā, 40th Master of the Naqshbandi-Haqqani Golden Chain. In his will, Grandshaykh ʿAbdAllāh predicted Shaykh Nazim would open Naqshbandi centers in the United Kingdom and bring traditional Islam to Europe. Fulfilling the order of his shaykh, Mawlana Shaykh Nazim traveled to London in 1974 without knowing a soul there or relying on anyone. Within a few short years he established a broad following of native Muslims and converts from the U.K. and Europe.

As a global melting pot, London was the perfect backdrop to reach people from around the world. In the late 1970s and throughout the 1980's, Shaykh Nazim traveled the Middle East, Europe, Southeast Asia, and the Pacific Rim. By 1980, three large mosques and a major Naqshbandi center at St. Anne's served as the growing multi-cultured group's western base in London, while Cyprus remained its eastern base.

In 1991, Shaykh Nazim sent his son-in-law, Shaykh Hisham Kabbani, to represent him in the United States. By 1995, fifteen Naqshbandi centers were established throughout the U.S. and Canada, attracting thousands of native Muslims and converts, providing them a peaceful, tolerant, loving alternative to the growing Islamist rhetoric that permeated mosques and Islamic centers. Shaykh Nazim visited the U.S. regularly in the 1990s.

Mawlana Shaykh Nazim is "al-Haqqani" meaning, "the truthful one." He is ranked among the top fifty in the ground-breaking book compiled by Georgetown University, *The 500 Most Influential Muslims—2009.* He has no trouble speaking truth to power and has addressed high offices of the United Nations and U.S. Congress. In June 2010, he was the sole Muslim leader to meet with His Holiness, Pope Benedict XVI, during the pontiff's visit to Cyprus. Shaykh Nazim's millions of followers include royalty, heads of state, high-level politicians, celebrities, industrialists, religious leaders, and common folk.

Grandshaykh ʿAbdAllāh's teachings and divine inspirations remain a constant in Mawlana Shaykh's Nazim's daily broadcast, breathing further life into his universal message: to love and serve the Creator, Allāh Almighty, to remain vigilant against those who deny Him, and to support good and avoid evil. Every year tens of thousands of faithful visit Mawlana Shaykh Nazim in Lefke, Cyprus, to seek his blessing, spiritual protection, and heavenly intercession.

The Sufilive Series is intended to bring you, dear reader, to Mawlana Shaykh Nazim's illumined presence. May your burdens be lifted and your heart filled with love, peace, happiness and spiritual devotion from these sacred, uplifting words. *Amīn.*

Preface

The *Sufilive Series* is based on transcripts of the *suḥbah,* extemporaneous, divinely inspired discourses, broadcast on the popular website, Sufilive.com. This volume is devoted to *suḥbah* of Mawlana Shaykh Nazim al-Haqqani.

Sufilive is the brainchild of Mawlana Shaykh Nazim's representative, Mawlana Shaykh Hisham Kabbani. Shaykh Hisham's undying effort to bring his aging spiritual guide to a global audience was realized in June 2009, with the momentous launch of a daily live broadcast from the elder shaykh's base in the remote town of Lefke, Cyprus. Although faced with a myriad of technical and other hurdles, by mid-summer the daily broadcast in English became a regular fixture on Sufilive, attracting hundreds of thousands of viewers and reaching people of all walks of life.

With Shaykh Hisham's support, a dozen staff maintain the free-membership website, which features live and recorded broadcasts and an extensive archive of discourses on a host of topics. One-hundred volunteer transcriptionists, translators, and editors from around the world help publish Mawlana Shaykh Nazim's discourses in English, Arabic, Turkish, Bahasa (Malay), Bahasa (Indo), Urdu, Farsi, French, German, Spanish, Italian, Dutch, Bosnian, Russian and Cantonese!

Our deep appreciation goes to the hard-working team of English transcribers and editors from across the U.S., Canada, U.K. and Europe, whose valuable contributions have made this collection a reality.

From his life of divine servanthood, in daily life and in these holy broadcasts, Mawlana Shaykh Nazim calls people back to their Lord, our heavenly Creator. He loves and respects all people, regardless of their chosen faith or lack thereof. We hope *The Sufilive Series* reflects this spirit.

Publisher's Notes

This book is directed to those familiar with the Sufi Way; however, to accommodate lay readers unfamiliar with Sufi terminology and practices, we have provided English translations of Arabic texts and a comprehensive glossary. Where Arabic terms are crucial to the discussion, we have included transliteration and footnoted explanations. For readers familiar with Arabic and Islamic teachings, for further clarity please consult the cited sources.

The original material is based on transcripts of a series of holy gatherings which serve as conduits of heavenly guidance. The *ṣuḥbah,* a divinely inspired talk which conveys powerful energy that uplifts the soul, is delivered by the "shaykh," a highly trained spiritual guide. To present the authentic flavor of such rare teachings, great care was taken to preserve the speaking styles of both the author and the illustrious shaykhs upon whose notes this book is based.

Translations from Arabic to English pose unique challenges which we have tried our best to make understandable to Western readers. In addition, please note the worldwide cultural practice to not include the definite article "the," as in "~~the~~ Prophet," which is a more intimate reference that appears occasionally throughout this work.

Quotes from the Holy Qur'an are offset, with chapter number and verse cited. The Holy Traditions of Prophet Muḥammad (*āḥadīth)* are offset and cited, in most cases. Historic dates are often referenced as "Hijri" and "A.H." (After Hijri), which is the commencement of the Islamic calendar, when Prophet Muḥammad migrated from Mecca to Madinah in 622 C.E. (Christian Era) to escape religious persecution and form his early nation. A reference calendar has also been provided.

Where gender-specific pronouns such as "he" and "him" are applied in a general sense, no discrimination is intended towards women, upon whom The Almighty bestowed great honor.

Islamic teachings are primarily based on four sources, in this order:

℘ **Holy Qur'an**: the holy book of divine revelation (God's Word) granted to Prophet Muḥammad. Reference to Holy Qur'an appears as "4:12," indicating "Chapter 4, Verse 12."

- **Sunnah**: holy traditions of Prophet Muḥammad ﷺ; the systematic recording of his words and actions that comprise the *ḥadīth*. For fifteen centuries, Islam has applied a strict, highly technical standard, rating each narration in terms of its authenticity and categorizing its "transmission." As this book is not highly technical, we simplified the reporting of *ḥadīth*, but included the narrator and source texts to support the discussion at hand.
- ***Ijma*ʿ**: The adherence, or agreement of the experts of independent reasoning *(āhl al-ijtihād)* to the conclusions of a given ruling pertaining to what is permitted and what is forbidden after the passing of the Prophet, Peace be upon him, as well as the agreement of the Community of Muslims concerning what is obligatorily known of the religion with its decisive proofs. Perhaps a clearer statement of this principle is, "We do not separate (in belief and practice) from the largest group of the Muslims."
- **Legal Rulings:** highly trained Islamic scholars form legal rulings from their interpretation of the Qur'an and the Sunnah, known as *ijtihād*. Such rulings are intended to provide Muslims an Islamic context regarding contemporary social norms. In theological terms, scholars who form legal opinions have completed many years of rigorous training and possess degrees similar to a doctorate in divinity in Islamic knowledge, or in legal terms, hold the status of a high court or supreme court judge, or higher.

The following universally recognized symbols have been respectfully included in this work. While they may seem tedious, they are deeply appreciated by a vast majority of our readers.

ﷻ *subḥānahu wa taʿala* (may His Glory be Exalted), recited after the name "Allāh" and any of the Islamic names of God.

ﷺ *ṣallAllāhu ʿalayhi wa sallam* (God's blessings and greetings of peace be upon him), recited after the holy name of Prophet Muḥammad.

عليه السلام *ʿalayhi ʿs-salām* (peace be upon him/her), recited after holy names of other prophets, names of Prophet Muḥammad's relatives, the pure and virtuous women in Islam, and angels.

رضي الله عنه/رضي الله عنها *raḍīAllāhu ʿanh(um)* (may God be pleased with him/her), recited after the holy names of Companions of Prophet Muḥammad; plural: *raḍīAllāhu ʿanhum.*

ق represents *qaddasAllāhu sirrah* (may God sanctify his secret), recited after names of saints.

Transliteration

Transliteration from Arabic to English poses challenges. To show respect, Muslims often capitalize nouns which, in English, normally appear in lowercase. To facilitate authentic pronunciation of names, places and terms, use the following key:

Symbol	Transliteration	Symbol	Transliteration	Vowels: Long	
ء	ʾ	ط	ṭ	آ ى	ā
ب	b	ظ	ẓ	و	ū
ت	t	ع	ʿ	ي	ī
ث	th	غ	gh	**Short**	
ج	j	ف	f	َ	**a**
ح	ḥ	ق	q	ُ	**u**
خ	kh	ك	k	ِ	**i**
د	d	ل	l		
ذ	dh	م	m		
ر	r	ن	n		
ز	z	ه	h		
س	s	و	w		
ش	sh	ي	y		
ص	ṣ	ة	ah; at		
ض	ḍ	ال	**al-/'l-**		

Foreword by Shaykh Hisham Kabbani

Aʿūdhu billāhi min ash-Shaytāni 'r-rajīm. Bişmillāhi 'r-Raḥmāni 'r-Raḥīm.
Madad yā Sulṭān al-Awlīyā, Shaykh Muḥammad Nāẓim al-Ḥaqqānī.
Madad yā Sulṭān al-Awlīyā, Shaykh ʿAbdAllāh al-Fā'iz ad-Dāghestānī.

No *madad,* no support; no *madad,* no talk; no *madad,* no energy; no *madad,* no provisions; no *madad,* no wealth; no *madad,* no health; no *madad,* nothing will happen. With *madad,* things change. If we leave the matter to us, without their support we will be like the others. We hope that all human beings will come to this door, the door of *awlīyāullāh,* and door of Sayyidīna Muḥammad ﷺ in order to be supported.

Technology is improving. Day by day it is changing. You cannot say you want to go back to 1950. I was in university in the late sixties; we had a course on IBM machines, the computer of that time. One computer needed three times more space than this room, and it only produced a punched card which you have to take to another computer to read. You don't want to go back to that. Now you are using a very fast laptop and everyday there is newer technology. If that is for *dunyā,* what is for the divine message?

You cannot compare what Sayyidīna Adam ﷺ and Sayyidīna Nuh ﷺ came with; Sayyidīna Nuh ﷺ was given much more of the heavenly message, different from what was given to Sayyidīna Adam ﷺ. Sayyidīna Adam was given what was necessary for his time and Sayyidīna Nuh ﷺ was given what was necessary for his time, different software and different knowledge.

The level of the prophets is not the same. What Sayyidīna Adam ﷺ was given is different from what Sayyidīna Nuh ﷺ was given and what he was given was different from what Sayyidīna Ibrahim ﷺ was given. As we move forward, everything is improving. Lifestyles in the time of Sayyidīna Nuh ﷺ were different than lifestyles in the time of Sayyidīna ʿIbrahim ﷺ. It changed. Sayyidīna ʿIbrahim ﷺ was given different from what Sayyidīna Mūsa ﷺ was given. Similarly, what Sayyidīna ʿIsa ﷺ was given was different from what Sayyidīna Muḥammad ﷺ was given. Sayyidīna Muḥammad ﷺ was given the highest, most perfect, heavenly technology or heavenly system. That is why we don't see any prophet after him ﷺ.

So why go back to the IBM computer? It filled a huge room and gave very limited information compared to a computer of today that connects you everywhere. Today computers and the Internet give you a very important idea that we have to think about. SubḥānAllāh, how everything has been connected through that Internet! Every human being is connected today through one system, so they can communicate with each other. So there must be a main server that connects everything.

Allāh ﷻ gave human beings the know-how of a main server so that everyone could be connected. Does He not have a server, an indescribable dome, a *qubbah*? For everything, every little atom in this universe, Allāh created a dome that connects the smallest atom of any species, any mineral, or any living or non-living element with the other. All of them speak. When you have many organizations, you go under one umbrella organization, a "holding company." That organization is holding many different companies and all are connected to the main holding company, the main server.

All of Creation is all connected to the main heavenly dome that is called by *awlīyāullāh*, Qubbat al-Arzāq, "the Dome of Provisions." Provision does not mean just food, but anything that Allāh ﷻ gave to this universe. So what do you think about that dome which is the umbrella of everything, the main connection through which people interact with each other? Each *walī* has a server which connects those connected to him under that dome. The other *walī* has another dome. That is why in the Holy Hadīth, Prophet ﷺ says, "My saints are under my domes." That means every *walī* has a dome, a connection.

There are big domes and small domes. Sayyīdā Maryam ؑ had a small dome. They asked Mawlana Shaykh what does "dome, dome" mean, what he is singing these days after the *suḥbah*. O listeners and viewers, you have to know what Mawlana Shaykh means. Allāh ﷻ gave each *walī* a dome, and all of them are under the main dome given to Sayyidīna Muḥammad ﷺ. He is calling you through "dome, dome" to say you are all under that heavenly dome! As much as he mentions it, Mawlana's heavenly singing is asking to open your "dome" for you. It is because his students, his *murīds* will be domes for others on the Day of Judgment, like you see shining stars on a dark night!

Murīds of the Naqshbandi-Haqqani Order, and others (we speak of our *ṭarīqah,* they can speak of theirs, it is up to them) will be like shining stars. They can be identified easily, wherever they are. The Prophet ﷺ said, "My Companions are like stars; whichever of them you follow, you will be rightly guided." *Awlīyāullāh* say, "Our students are like stars." They are not the same ranks as the *Saḥābah* ﷺ, but still they are shining stars. The Companions' stars cannot be imagined; they are huge. But the students of *awlīyāullāh* are small shining stars also. Do you want to be a big star or a small star? *Awlīyā's* understanding is that the big stars are *murīds* that come and listen to the shaykh through a representative or through the Internet. Prophet ﷺ said, "My saints are under my domes," and, "My Companions are like stars; whichever of them you follow, you will be guided."

Awlīyāullāh inherited a secret from the Prophet ﷺ. There are 124,000 *awlīyāullāh* and 124,000 *Saḥābah*. Even a small child who saw the Prophet ﷺ is considered a Companion, so it means any star. Even if you had followed that child that saw the Prophet ﷺ just once, it was enough for your happiness all your life. But how can one see? Because through that child's eyes are the eyes of the Prophet ﷺ. Who looked into his eyes saw the Prophet ﷺ, and this is how the Muḥammadan Light was dispatched. That light is constantly moving at the speed of 300 kilometers per second. The light Prophet ﷺ is sending to the *ummah* never dies.

So Prophet ﷺ said, from Allāh ﷻ saying to him, "My saints are under my domes." It means that everyone was given a dome like Sayyīdā Maryam ؏. She found provisions; they will find provisions, both physical and spiritual. They are not in need of people. Allāh makes people to serve the *awlīyā*. Don't think if the shaykh supports you he will let you down. All of you are supported, or else you wouldn't come to these associations. All followers of Mawlana Shaykh are supported. If not, they would not listen nor would they care.

Allow me to mention, if a politician makes an important speech on TV, everyone will stop what they are doing to see that message. TV networks and Internet sites send that around the world and broadcast it live. Millions of people listen to that worldly speech, because they want to know how it will impact them. What do you think about someone who is taking you to the heart of Sayyidīna Muḥammad ﷺ and speaking to you from that ocean?! Don't think Mawlana Shaykh is sitting in his chair, speaking like everyone else. He is connected to that ocean and you are connected through him.

Don't miss that live broadcast, as the heavenly one is sending heavenly messages through it, which raises you higher and higher! For those who do not watch (without a good excuse), Shaytān is making them deaf and blind. The dome of Sayyidīna Muḥammad ﷺ, the Dome of Provision, Qubbat al-

Arzāq, provides you with all kinds of information about how you will behave and improve your moral excellence, and it gives secrets to your heart that you never heard before! And where are you when this live broadcast is being transmitted? We say to ourselves that we will listen and hear it later. But at that moment the *tajāllī* and blessings are coming! If you watch live, you get it. If you watch the recording later, you will get only some of it, and not as intense.

Sayyidīna Imām Abū Hamid al-Ghazali ق, one of the great scholars of tasawwuf and Shari'ah, was like every other scholar before he became open-hearted. However, he had doubts; whisperings also came to his heart. When *ināyatullāh,* Allāh's divine care, comes, that is what counts. You don't know when it will come so you have to observe continuously and be ready always, seeking that precise moment it will appear. Just as they go to the beach to sight the moon for Ramadan, and just at the last moment when the sun sets, they seek out the moon. Also the *awlīyāullāh* seek out the appropriate time when Allāh's divine care is coming in order to "jump" into it.

One day, Imām al-Ghazāli ق was sitting as usual, writing; however, that day he had to write an important letter to save someone who was to be hanged or tortured. A fly sat on the inkwell. When Allāh ﷻ wants His divine care to reach someone it may reach in any moment, but you have to be ready for it. He said to himself, "Allāh ﷻ created that fly and He created me as well, and we are both created from the light of Muḥammad ﷺ. Tonight is the Prophet's birthday, *laylat al-ithnayn,* so I will leave that fly to suck the ink for the sake of Mawlid an-Nabī."

That was the Night of Divine Care, and Imām al-Ghazāli ق reached it; he was ready for it. You don't know when it may come, but you have to prepare yourself. So that night, he let the fly drink the ink for love of the Sayyidīna Muḥammad ﷺ. Allāh liked that and His divine care opened an ascension on Imām al-Ghazali, not because he studied scholarly material, no; it was because of that small action. When that station is opened the divine care will reach you; not on your own time but on their heavenly time. When you are ready and waiting, waiting, waiting, any moment it can reach you.

Sufilive.com offers an on-demand library of recorded talks. Many people view them later, but it is more important to see the live broadcast, as that heavenly station is open then.

Those who translate and transcribe what comes from that dome of knowledge, don't think you are not being rewarded! For every letter you write, Allāh ﷻ is opening 12,000 oceans of knowledge from the secret of Mawlana's request for you, as you have the dedication to write and translate his teachings to make them accessible for others. If you increase the languages translated, his message will reach more people.

Qubbat al-Arzāq, the Dome of Provisions, is the main source of heavenly secrets sent to the people's hearts. One way to explain this is like when you archive your emails and retrieve them later. Do you think *awlīyāullāh* don't have emails, inspirations they send to your heart? When you are not available they keep sending and your heart archives them, saving those inspirations. When *awlīyāullāh* open that for you, you receive that inspiration, and at that time you submit to Allāh ﷻ. There you don't see your ego; you are clean. Then they will show you what they archived to your heart over many years, all the inspirations they sent so that one day you will retrieve them. That dome is *baḥr muhīt*, an all-encompassing ocean!

We are blessed and also excited to offer *The Sufilive Series*, a collection of transcripts of live broadcasts, one more invitation to jump into the Dome of Provision that awaits.

Wa min Allāhī 't-tawfiq, bī ḥurmati 'l-ḥabīb, bī ḥurmati 'l-Fātiḥah.
And with Allāh is success. For the sake of the Beloved, for his sake we recite the opening chapter of Holy Qur'an.

Masters of the Naqshbandi-Haqqani Golden Chain

1. Prophet Muḥammad ibn ʿAbdAllāh ﷺ
2. Abū Bakr aṣ-Ṣiddīq ق
3. Salmān al-Farsi ق
4. Qasim bin Muḥammad bin Abū Bakr ق
5. Jafar as-Ṣādiq ق
6. Tayfur Abū Yazid al-Bistāmī ق
7. Abūl Hassan ʿAlī al-Kharqani ق
8. Abū ʿAlī al-Farmadi ق
9. Abū Yaqub Yusuf al-Hamadani ق
10. Abūl Abbas, al-Khidr ق
11. ʿAbdul Khaliq al-Ghujdawani ق
12. Arif ar-Riwakri ق
13. Khwaja Mahmoud al-Anjir al-Faghnawi ق
14. ʿAlī ar-Ramitani ق
15. Muḥammad Baba as-Samasi ق
16. as-Sayyid Amir Kulal ق
17. Muḥammad Bahaʿuddin Shah Naqshband ق
18. Alaʿuddin al-Bukhāri al-Attar ق
19. Yaqūb al-Charkhi ق
20. Ubaydullāh al-Ahrar ق
21. Muḥammad az-Zahid ق
22. Darwish Muḥammad ق
23. Muḥammad Khwaja al-Amkanaki ق
24. Muḥammad al-Baqi bilLah ق
25. Aḥmad al-Farūqi as-Sirhindi ق
26. Muḥammad al-Masum ق
27. Muḥammad Sayfuddin al-Farūqi al-Mujaddidi ق
28. as-Sayyid Nūr Muḥammad al-Badawani ق
29. Shamsuddin Habib Allāh ق
30. AbdAllāh ad-Dahlawi ق
31. Khalid al-Baghdadi ق
32. Ismaīl Muḥammad ash-Shirwāni ق
33. Khas Muḥammad Shirwāni ق
34. Muḥammad Effendi al-Yaraghi ق
35. Jamaluddin al-Ghumuqi al-Husayni ق
36. Abū Aḥmad as-Sughuri ق
37. Abū Muḥammad al-Madani ق
38. Sharafuddīn ad-Daghestani ق
39. ʿAbdAllāh al-Faʿiz ad-Daghestani
40. Muḥammad Nazim Adil al-Haqqani ق

Seek Eternity and Limitless Paradises

A'ūdhu billāhi min ash-Shaytāni 'r-rajīm. Bismillāhi 'r-Raḥmāni 'r-Raḥīm. Dastūr, yā Sayyidī. Madad, yā rijālAllāh!

Stand up for your Lord's glory! *Allāhu Akbar, Allāhu Akbar, lā ilāha illa-Llāh, Allāhu Akbar, Allāhu Akbar, wa lillāhi 'l-ḥamd!* All praising and all glory is for our Lord, Almighty Allāh, and presented to His most beloved and honored one in His Divine Presence, also glory and honor! May Allāh ﷻ forgive us. We are asking for forgiveness, O our Lord, and asking for Your blessings. We are so weak ones, asking endlessly salutes and greetings for Your most beloved one in Your Divine Presence, Sayyidīna Muḥammad ﷺ. *Yā Rabb!*

O People! *As-salāmu 'alaykum.* That *salām* gives you *salāmat*, safety, here and Hereafter. Give some time for listening to heavenly announcements, because if you are listening and accepting, just taken over from your sufferings and miseries. And we are looking that everyone now is drowning in sufferings and miseries. Therefore, if you are asking *hayyātun tayyibah*, to live a good life here for a period granted to you, to be here in safety and in happiness and enjoyment, then you must say, *As-salāmu 'alaykum,* salute on believers from their Lord. That is one of the biggest grants of our Lord to take away heavy burdens from our shoulders!

O People! We are saying because we have been ordered to be in connection with heavenly beings, holy ones. Holiness is not by dressing in strange clothes or wearing something exotic on your heads, no. Holiness is a grant put on your head like crowns for kings or emperors. Ask for that holiness that Allāh Almighty sends through His prophets, peace be upon them, and to who follow their ways. There is a way reaching to holy stations and there is another way that carries people to sewage channels. Therefore, holy people who are asking to reach the level of holiness are getting much more care and they are scared to fall into sewage channels. That is a way.

All prophets taught about the Day of Resurrection, when the Lord of Heavens gives His majestic judgment on the people crowded there. After being under divine judgment, they will be ordered, "Now walk!" and everyone will reach their individual places or areas where they will remain forever. Now you are walking, and then they are walking on a very thin and very difficult bridge over fire. Who can pass on it will reach Paradise, and their Lord's pleasure, honor, and happiness! That is granted to them after passing on that bridge. That is the way of holy ones, who keep their steps in this life on holy ways; they will be able to pass over that very thin, very sharp, and very terrible bridge. But that is the way of those who, in their lives, prefer to walk on the ways of holy ones. They will pass over that holy bridge, reaching up to holy lands granted from the Lord of Heavens, and no one knows its limits!

SubḥānAllāh! Glory to Allāh Almighty! According to holy books, the last one entering Paradise is granted ten times like this planet if you are making flat, and he will be so happy. But more than that happiness, he was thinking, "If this territory is in limits, what about if I will be here forever? Do you think that I can be happy with an imitated paradise up to Eternal?" Something was coming to his heart. The last one entering thinking, "What is ten times of this world?" Now it is so big for a person living here, but the Lord giving to that person that he may be remembering and asking, "O my Lord, our life in *dunyā* was in limits because our lives in limit, but here unlimited, Eternal life. If You are granting us Eternal life, this ten times *dunyā* is nothing! We are looking more from Your Majesty and Your majestic kingdom with never-ending dominions and oceans of Creation!"

Inhabitants of Paradise are saying, "We are so big and this is nothing! We are asking, and we hope this not only for us. With happiness we are hoping this Paradise must be as a sea and if growing, it is getting a tree, and from that tree in that garden taking seeds from fruits and making it more!"

A divine address to them, "O My servant! Now be happy what I am granting to you. Don't try to teach Me. Don't try what I am asking to give to you a limit. Everything in Eternity is Eternal. O My servant! (I am granting to you) that world ten times daily, ten times Paradise that I granted to you! Second day it will be double, third day you will find three times, fourth day you will find four times bigger! Be happy, in contentment. Don't worry, I am the Lord! Don't try to teach Me something. I am granting to you. Now today you are entering and you are seeing a big land, ten times of world, and tomorrow you will find it double ten times more, and third day you are going to find it thirty times bigger! O My servant! Enjoy My endless favors!"

O People! That is a holy way. If anyone of you asking to reach those holy lands that day-by-day getting more and more, don't think that it is going (to be only) three times bigger. When it is granted three times as the first grant, second day going to be twenty times, and third day from twenty times going to be ten times more. What is it going to be? Two-hundred times, and two-hundred times making it double. Fourth day you are going to find two-hundred times, four-hundred times bigger.

"My Lord, if I can reach to that?"

"If you are not reaching, how you are asking? What I granted to you, I know it. You will be happy, and more happy. You are not going to say, 'enough'; always you are going to say, *hal min mazīd,* 'O my Lord, I am asking for more; I am not getting full from Your grants. O my Lord, give more and more and more.'"

O People! That is something that coming to me for declaring to all nations and all people. Mostly people now on this Earth are just mixed with miseries and sufferings; no taste for their lives, no one getting a pleasure for their permanent temporary life. You are never taking any taste.

O People! Our Lord is calling us. Why are you not giving? Why are you not trying to give daily even five minutes for your Lord, Almighty Allāh, for thanking and making *sajdah* for Him and thanking to your Lord? What is that foolishness from you? What is that ignorance from you? What is that your dirtiness? So big, you are like rats living in sewage channels and not asking to get out. Why? And every day sufferings getting more and more on your shoulders and you are young ones beginning to come down, down, down. This is a very important message from heavenly levels.

O People! That is a warning as well as it is endlessly good tidings for you! Give some minutes for your Lord, for His pleasure, then He grants to you endlessly pleasure here and Hereafter. Ohhh, drinking in pubs, drinking in casinos, drinking in bad places, and doing dirty things! It is not your honor, O Man, to do bad things! It is not honor of a deputy to take dirty things! It is blame to Mankind that they are only thinking how they are killing people, how they are giving trouble to people, how getting more trouble to people! That is your humanity? "*Ptuu* (spit)" on such a humanity! Allāh takes away who are killing and giving trouble because divine anger is approaching because you are living and reaching the last station of this planet and the Day of Resurrection is just approaching. You will be ashamed, most ashamed on the Day of Resurrection.

O People! Leave drinking alcohol because drunkenness is under the level of donkeys. Actually, a donkey is never happy to drink beer, so how will I be happy to drink it? Arabs are also drinking. What are they drinking? *Arak,* I know. You are Arab and not knowing. Making from dates and drinking. In Egypt making from dates and drinking. Turks now they are free, drinking everything, whatever coming they are drinking. Then? When a person drinking, no more their minds working; finished. When their minds are not working, they are cut off from humanity and reaching to level under the level of animals, because animals are not drinking. Leave to be drunk ones! Then one day you will be unhappy. Give some times for thinking, to learn for your beginning and for your end.

O People! May Allāh ﷻ forgive us. We are only asking that someone will be sent from Heavens to correct our steps and the time is over for that one coming and Jesus Christ coming and then going to be Judgment Day! Keep your honor, O Mankind! Leave bad customs and try to reach good customs from holy ones because if no holy one, no way to Eternal life, no Eternity for them.

May Allāh forgive us, for the honor of most honored one in His Divine Presence, Sayyidīna Muḥammad ﷺ. *Yā Rasūlullāh*!

Those are happy sounds from Heavens coming to good ones hearing. Hear and listen, and enjoy with divine singings and music. You will be happy here and Hereafter. O our Lord, forgive us!

Don't be angry with me, O People! I am asking for your happiness here and Hereafter, and I am asking for your pleasure in the Divine Presence that gives you endless honor with prophets, holy ones, and angels! Try to be with them, not in sewage channels with rats and *shaytans*. May Allāh protect us.

May Allāh ﷻ forgive us.

Fātiḥah.

Holy Commands Bring Endless Contentment

A'ūdhu billāhi min ash-Shaytāni 'r-rajīm. Biṣmillāhi 'r-Raḥmāni 'r-Raḥīm.
Dastūr, yā Sayyidī. Madad, yā rijālAllāh!

Yā Rabbī, shukr! Dastūr, yā Sulṭān al-Awlīyā. Stand up all creatures! All creatures on Earth now are standing up following me, and I am the weakest servant standing up! They are standing up for the honor of our Lord, our Creator, Allāh Almighty! *Allāhu Akbar, Allāhu Akbar, lā ilāha illa-Llāh, Allāhu Akbar, Allāhu Akbar, wa lillāhi 'l-ḥamd! Allāhu Akbar khabīra, w 'alḥamdūlillāhi 'l-kathīra, wa SubḥānAllāhi 'l-'Adhīm wa bi-ḥamdihi 'l-Karīm bukratan wa asīla! Lā ilāha illa-Llāh, Allāhu Akbar, Allāhu Akbar, wa lillāhi 'l-ḥamd!*

O People! Hear and listen, and obey your Lord's holy commands. If you are asking to have an honor, you must give your highest honor for His Divine Presence. And you must give honor to the most glorified and honored one in His Divine Presence, Sayyidīna Muḥammad ﷺ. Anyone asking to reach our Lord's Mercy Oceans must give much honor and glory to the most glorified and honored one in His Divine Presence, Sayyidīna Muḥammad ﷺ.

O People! *As-salāmu 'alaykum wa raḥmatūllahi wa barakātuh.* We are asking for you goodness! We are asking for you blessings! We are not against you, O People! Don't think that any holy ones will be against common people. And we are saying, *a'ūdhu billāhi min ash-Shaytāni 'r-rajīm. Bismillāhi 'r-Raḥmāni 'r-Raḥīm.*

We are running away from Shaytān and *shaytanic* efforts, because Shaytān asking to give the servants of our Lord, as much as it can do, trouble and sufferings and miseries: that is Shaytān's mission. The Lord of Heavens takes him away. I am ashaming to call Allāh Almighty for the reason of Shaytān and saying, "O our Lord, take Shaytān away from us!"

O People! Even a small ant and smaller than an ant, a virus, may take Shaytān away. I am saying 'virus' that belongs to the level of Shaytān. I am not speaking about the virus that is running around on this planet, running around living ones, no. I am saying 'virus' that is on the level of Shaytān. That is another kind; that 'virus' is not the same virus that is surrounding this planet. It is another kind, because Allāh Almighty, the Creator, can create everything as He likes. No one preventing our Lord to create or to do something!

Beware, O Mankind, from your Lord's heavy punch to come on this planet and make it down and disappear. Divinely punch not like such a planet; if divinely punch reaching, all space that we are looking at and wondering about, making that to be crushed, finished! He is Allāh Almighty ﷻ! O People! Fear from your Lord, Allāh Almighty! Come and listen, come and be obedient ones or sending on you some viruses to take you away and not in one day, not one hour, not in minutes or seconds, but smaller than a second's time; may take everything from existence, to be nothing in existence!

Fear from your Lord, and try to be respectful for His holy commands. Take heavenly commands with the most respect and don't take heavenly commands lightly. Don't take holy commands in such a way that you never giving respect! You must give your most high respect for His commands and you must say, "We are hearing and obeying, O our Lord!"

O our Lord! O Allāh! We are so, so weak. You are so great, majestic, and so glorified! Your dominions are countless and through them there are countless oceans of life. He is Hayy; His existence is from Himself! No one is giving our Lord to be in existence, but He is that One, Who is giving life for all Creation. By His command comes life for everything. It is only enough for our Lord to say, "Be!" and it comes to exist.

I am ashaming to say this for our Lord, because His Greatness is endless! But that word, one of His chosen, holy ones may say according to the heavenly order, "Come and be alive," and life may come. But I am saying this for making a clarification for people about Allāh Almighty giving life, saying, "Living ones, be alive!" He is so high, Allāh Almighty, so great. All Creation and all creatures in His Divine Presence are never going more than a *dharrah*, atom; it means they are nothing!

He has Real Being but everything is never granted a real being. Absolute Reality is for the Lord of Heavens, for the Lord of All Creation, and His creation is never-ending. When it began and when it will finish, no one knows except Him. Understand? What does it mean, "finish?" Don't say, "I am this one, I am that one."

O Mankind! Try to learn good manners, particularly good manners for your Creator. Be a good one with your *adab*. That is also one of the biggest pleasures and good tidings for Mankind. Such words signify something about Eternity. No one, even prophets, can bring a real description or explanation about Eternity. Eternity, Eternity. Therefore, Allāh Almighty, He is only One, can't be a second one. He is only One in Himself. No one is helping Him to be in existence, but He is giving existence countlessly to everything from pre-Eternal, and no one can know what is the meaning of *azāl* and *abād*, pre-Eternal and Eternal. *Allāhu Akbar*!

O People! Such words, such explanation, they are granting now through such an instrument, asking to reach to everyone; with some knowledge as a foundation. Because coming days bringing something for Man; that 'something' needs a foundation. Coming a new understanding, a new page opening in Creation. Because every day there is another appearance; today's appearance never the same as tomorrow. Therefore, your understanding about Eternity going on endlessly and never finishing. That is from our Lord; a countless grant to Mankind, that they have been appointed through all Creation to be his deputies. Perhaps everything, they have something from knowledge about their Creator.

Therefore, everything according to their understanding making *tasbeeh*, glorifying for their Lord with their different languages. Everything, they are giving glorifying for their Creator. Daily that is changing also. Today's glorifying is different from yesterday, and for tomorrow, glorifying of that creature just changing. It is another grant from their Creator: to give their glorifying for their Lord, not on same words. No, they are changing, just changing. Do you think if a person invites the sulṭān, everyday putting beans on his table, daily, daily, daily? Therefore, everything in existence, they have a special name with special appearance, with special understanding, daily. And every day they are giving most high glorifying to their Lord, daily.

Therefore, Prophet ﷺ was saying, "O People! think about yourselves, your being, but don't try to think and to learn something about your Lord's Absolute Being." Understand? Where we are? We are so weak ones, but daily coming new things to make our lights more clear, lighter and brightened. And that one, getting much more honor through glorifying their Lord. When a creature giving his or its glorifying to their Lord, their Lord granting them something else. Some more honor and lights and brightness and endless grants coming from Heavens.

Therefore, we are saying, if Allāh Almighty asking for anything to come in existence, He is saying, 'Be' and it is coming. They are speaking on that point that from everyone in existence, highest level through creation granted to Mankind, beyond Mankind. We have been honored to be our Lord's deputies, but deputies' levels also countless. You are deputy, he is deputy, that is deputy, but his deputy-being is just different from that one and yours just different. And levels of deputy coming countlessly, and this deputy, that Holy Qur'an saying about Adam, he has been created for this planet, and the Lord of Heavens glorifying him; *takrīm,* honoring him. But some holy ones, they are reaching high-level standards through Heavens. How many Heavens? They are seven Heavens; that is *mandhūma,* a system that belongs to this Creation. Beyond this, how much existence that keeping honor of being deputy? How many kinds of deputies? This is impossible for one Adam, that created being and his generation. They are deputies, but they full, 100% deputies; those are deputies of Allāh. It is so impossible, therefore, countless creations are created for being their Lords' deputies.

Therefore, some *awlīyā* saying that the number of *'alam,* universes, Adam is one. But like Adam and his universe, what opening coming to some real knowing ones through their being deputies, is that 124,000 Adams just passed away and our grandfather Adam was the last one from 124,000 Adams. And nothing preventing Allāh Almighty to create more than this, but this is only according to our capacity. So that such an explanation or understanding now coming to people that they may understand something about Who is the Creator and what is His power. Don't be like such drunk people that said this universe was one atom and exploded and being this and that, Big Bang. They are so dirty and dirty-thinking. It is not a good explanation. No, no. Countless universes, with countless kinds of creatures and with countless deputies of their Lord. May Allāh ﷻ forgive us.

O People! Such things coming now to make your understanding wider, wider, wider. Because as much as you can understand, you can reach a contentment in yourself. Through contentment you are feeling like a person as if sitting in a hot place and refreshing weather comes; refreshment comes to people through such explanations, because they have been created to know more and more, more and more, more and more. And as much as they have been granted of their refreshment, their contentment, happiness, enjoyments and lightenings will be more and more, with such conditions that you can't add them.

O People! May Allāh ﷻ forgive us. We are wasting our times. Wasting our most precious grant from our Lord. Wasting, so that so many people remaining on the same level. Only such a people who are trying to understand what is granted to prophets, messengers and heavenly ones; they will have such a pleasure that no one can know. Only those who may taste it. O Allāh, forgive us for the honor of most honored one, Sayyidīna Muḥammad ﷺ. *Huuu,* in those worlds and universes such heavenly singings come that make a dead one stand up! We are only making an imitation.

Just we have been granted such an addressing to people because in the past times it was not opened, but the Last Days are so near that strange, very *ajā'īb,* unexpected knowledges and understandings will be open for people who are living on this planet! Make us, O Allāh, to understand something. *Tawbah yā Rabbī, tawbah yā Rabbī, tawbah yā Rabbī, tawbah astaghfirullāh. Shukr yā Rabbī.*

May Allāh ﷻ forgive us.

Fātiḥah.

Come to Learn Holy Knowledge!

A'ūdhu billāhi min ash-Shaytāni 'r-rajīm. Biṣmillāhi 'r-Raḥmāni 'r-Raḥīm. Dastūr, yā Sayyidī. Madad, yā rijālAllāh!

O People! Stand up for your Lord Allāh Almighty. All Creation is standing up in His Divine Presence! O People! Give your most high respect and glorifying to your Lord, our Creator. No one can be in existence if he is not creating.

Allāhu Akbar, Allāhu Akbar, lā ilāha illa-Llāh, Allāhu Akbar, Allāhu Akbar, wa lillāhi 'l-ḥamd! Allāhu Akbar Kabira wa 'l-ḥamdulillāhi kathīra wa subhānAllāhi 'l-'adhīm wa bī ḥamdihi 'l-karīm bukratan wa asīlah. O Allāh, for the honor of Your most honored one, in Your Divine Presence, forgive us. We are asking for Your blessings, O our Lord. Give the highest honor that you are granting anyone through Creation, Sayiddina Muḥammad ﷺ! Give him much more glory and praising. *Madad yā Sayyidī.*

And we are asking, *a'ūdhu billāhi min ash-Shaytāni 'r-rajīm. Bismillāhi 'r-Raḥmāni 'r-Raḥīm.* Try to learn the meaning of *a'ūdhu billāhi min ash-Shaytāni 'r-rajīm.* Try to know what is the power of *Bismillāhi 'r-Raḥmāni 'r-Raḥīm.* That is a heavenly, official language granted to the Seal of Prophets, Sayyidīna Muḥammad ﷺ! He is the king, the emperor, and no one can reach his level and his honor in the Divine Presence.

O People! *As-salāmu 'alaykum;* that is the highest honor that Man is granted in holy stations, to be addressed by the Holy Name of Allāh Almighty. He is *as-Salām, Jalla Jalāluhu. As-Salām* means that a person who is accepting and asking from his Creator's Holy Name *"as-Salām"* must be in safety here and Hereafter. *As-salām,* so honored addressing from Heavens to Mankind. Use that holy word. Leave saying, "good morning, good evening, *gunaydin."* Other people are also saying imitation greetings with no power in them. Shaytān is teaching people to use that, because it is such a plastic bone with nothing in it, only emptiness. They are using this as a *salām,* greeting. Yes, it is a greeting, but a heavenly greeting is full with energy or power or lightening. If you are using it, you may say an atom as a weapon, making a big destroying because it has something in it; it is not empty. Also *salām* has such a heavenly power. When you say, *As-salāmu 'alaykum,* that is a grant from Heavens to you. Heavens are for living ones; everything there is living, not sleeping or heedless like dead ones. Death is on this planet only, to take your imitated one from you and grant you a real life's lightening and power. It gives that to you.

Kullu man ʿalayha fān.

Everything on Earth will perish. 55:26

Holy words from Holy Qur'an. All of you are dead ones. In the blink of an eye you are disappearing. That is the real position for this planet. When you are leaving this and getting up, you will find there Eternity. Eternity is in Heavens, and all Creation on this planet is temporary.

O People! Try to reach higher worlds, to become heavenly beings. Don't be stupid, ignorant, heedless ones. You may lose the only chance you have been granted. Only once you will be in existence on this planet and you may choose your way, either Heavens or down. Heavenly levels are full with lightening, more and more and more.

Heavenly beings are taking from heavenly levels. They will be *yamuddūn,* provided from never-ending divine levels. That is the meaning of Eternity. Eternity never decreases, it increases!

O People! Ask for more and more and more; you will be granted! *SubḥānAllāh,* Glory to our Creator. He is sending that *salām* as a living atom, either taking you up or sending you down. That *salām,* we are making as an example, is like an atom, a living atom; living never getting to be un-living. Always living, because *yamuddūn,* each atom providing from Heavens. Every atom that we are asking to say, *as-salām. Salām* is such a living power. It is covered with heavenly cover. When you say, *As-salāmu ʿalaykum,* that *salām* touches you with refreshment and renewment for your physical being, because you have secret power. You are keeping that secret power, making you to move like this, like that. Every function you have been granted is from Heavens.

That is an atom. What I am asking to say, atom of *salām. As-salāmu ʿalaykum,* gives to you such a power that you can't imagine. That living, never-ending power takes you from the darkness of this planet up to lightening heavenly levels.

O People! It is something we have been granted! Only prophets have such a secret knowledge, and they came to teach people their levels, positions, and their *waziyat,* missions. Beware; don't lose that chance you have been granted. It may leave you and then you will be a carcass. Therefore, *as-salām qabl al-kalām.* The teacher of all Creation Sayyidīna

Muḥammad ﷺ was saying, "O People! first say *salām*, then speak." That giving to you a power from *salām*. *Salām* giving to your real being a power, through which you may reach *ma'arib, ma'arib*, what you are asking here or Hereafter. Here nothing, but you must ask something that it will be for Eternal (life).

O People! Always ask for Eternity, Eternity. Don't lose your chance for reaching Eternity. You can't find over that position to be an Eternal one. Try to be Eternal one. When you will be an Eternal one, what kind of grant going to be granted to you, you can't understand now. But try to reach that.

Yes, they are making a declaration for anyone. I'm a simple one also, but they are making me to speak. I don't know but they know and making to give such a *mu'adhdham*, magnificent positions, to people because time is now coming closer, closer, closer. Our planet is going to finish and how many people on it, are reaching their targets or to their limits. Some of them wasting their chance and reaching nothing. Some of them gaining or winning such a power that forever you are running through oceans of Eternity. Never going to get out.

You are not asking (for) original. If running through Eternity Oceans, no one asking to come out. Never. Their real life through Eternity oceans and time is over now. Allāh Almighty just sent 104 heavenly messages, commands, orders and holy books and finally Holy Qur'an. All these holy books bringing holy knowledge. They are asking now, we are in need of holy knowledge. The knowledge that Shaytān teaching people is finished. It is like sewage channels material. Never giving any benefit, for when they are changing this life to another life.

Now we are in need of holy knowledge. O People! O Pope! O Bishops! O Chief Rabbis! O Patriarchs! O Dalai Lama! Do you know this or not? If knowing, say to people, order them: O People! enough that you occupied your most valuable beings for nothing, for imitated, dirty things. O People! you have been created to reach holy knowledge. Now we are in need of holy knowledge. We must try to learn holy knowledge. If not, we will be carcasses and thrown through sewage channels, like rats. Come and learn. Ask holy knowledge; taking you up and up, seven levels of Heavens.

O People! enough you will be drunk, drinking whiskey, champagne, vodka, *nabit*. Don't drink cognac; don't drink whiskey, talky-walky, Johnny Walker. Finished. You will be in sewage channels. Come and try to learn holy knowledge.

O People! from the East to the West from North to South. Seventy-two kinds of nations; you must close your nonsense universities, academies and high schools. You must close them and open a new page for your life, to teach your youngsters. To teach them and to train them for holy knowledge. *Allāh, Allāh. Allāhu Akbar*!

O People! that is important, that they are giving tonight. Tonight is very holy night for all nations. Come and accept holiness of this night and come and accept the month of this Friday night. Holy night and holy month. Try to learn something. Leave everything and Allāh Almighty grants to you everything, you can't think on it or you can't imagine. O People! come and listen. I am an old one, I am nothing, but they are making me to address to all nations. Kings, queens and dictators, all of you! Come and learn holy knowledge. You will be saved and honored through this life and real life through Heavens. You may reach real life through Eternity, through Eternal life.

May Allāh ﷻ forgive us. This is an endless ocean. Therefore, how many nights they are making my tongue to speak, I don't know. They are giving an order to speak, to address all nations. I don't think that anyone may object on this when we are reminding people to learn heavenly language and holy knowledge. It gives you honor, pleasure, lightenings and enjoyment, here and Hereafter, forever! *Tawbah yā Rabbī, tawbah astaghfirullāh.*

May Allāh ﷻ forgive us.

Fātiḥah.

What Makes Humans Move

A'ūdhu billāhi min ash-Shaytāni 'r-rajīm. Biṣmillāhi 'r-Raḥmāni 'r-Raḥīm. Dastūr, yā Sayyidī. Madad, yā rijālAllāh!

As-salāmu 'alaykum. Ash-hadu anlā ilāha illa-Llah, wa ash-hadu anna Muḥammadan 'abduhu wa Rasūluh. In the Name of Allāh, the Most Beneficent and the Most Munificent.

We are saying to our listeners, *as-salāmu alaykum wa raḥmatūllahi wa barakatuh.* This association is simple, but it is not from myself, no; it is from heavenly ones. I am also asking to hear and listen as it is not something we have prepared to speak to people, but it is a heavenly association from those who are sending their power to weak servant. I am calling myself a servant, but I am not a real servant. I am ashaming to say I am a servant, because I am not giving real service for the Lord of Heavens!

We gave our oath to our Lord, Almighty Allāh, that we would be His servants, but when we came here, we were born into this planet we have shown such a weak servanthood. As I look throughout East and West, from north to south, I also see how people have forgotten their oath that have given in the Divine Presence on the Day of Oath when we said, "O our Lord! We are giving to Your Divinely Presence that we are Your servants and we will do only Your service."

That was our oath in the Divine Presence, which our souls gave. However, now that we are here, we are not keeping our oath. We are occupying ourselves with materials, and materials for real beings of Mankind in the Divine Presence is nothing. But we are only acting for our material being that day-by-day will melt.

Once I was on a tourist ship, showing its passengers so many places. Once after praying the morning prayer, I looked at the main hall of that ship and saw a statue. You can say I saw a very beautiful figure as I was passing. At evening time, I passed again and looked to find where was that beautiful figure I saw in the morning. One of the passengers said, "O Shaykh! It was not something from stone or from metal." From what, I wondered, because I was looking from far away. It was only a piece of ice! Therefore, it began to melt, melt, and kept melting slowly, and by evening it had melted away, becoming water.

Our Grandshaykh, Allāh bless him, was saying, "O Nazim Effendi! Everything that you are seeing is going to melt and will finally disappear. The figure you are looking at is not a stable figure, and everything on this planet is going to melt, particularly Mankind, whose figures are like that ice figure." Day-by-day it is going to melt and finally become water, without any figure able to look, hear or speak. That was a manmade figure, but our material being that our Lord created is also going to melt away as days go by, melting away some instruments that are working by a battery.

Once there was a Bedouin on his camel going from one place to another. At nighttime he reached to a full water well. He then took his rest and slept. Early morning he stood up and asked whether he will continue on his way or complete his journey. However, he looked at his camel that was no longer moving. He tried to make like this, to open its eyes, but its head fell down. Then he fell down on one side and went round saying, "O, what happened to my camel? I was riding on it and it was running through deserts as fast as the wind. What happened now? It is no longer looking, nor standing, nor carrying me. What happened? Which thing finished? What is now missing? Everything I am seeing seems okay, so what happened?"

As he was crying and going around, another passenger reached him and saw that Arab Bedouin shouting, "What happened to my camel? Yesterday it was running like the wind. What happened?"

That one told him, "O, you never met a death of someone?"

"What is that?"

"Yes, yesterday it was alive, and today it is a dead body."

"O my brother! But I am seeing nothing missing."

"Yes, that power is not from the material world; that was something coming from Heavens making that one to move, to run like wind."

"Haaa. Now I understand that it is not our bodies that we are taking. We are taking so much care for our physical being, and that one passed away from its heavenly connection and just finished and dying."

O Mankind! You are seeing that you are taking much more care, making now new modern people, asking to be like cars with every year new-fashion. Old fashion finishing and putting in cemetery for cars. And you are finishing. You can bring new-fashion car, but you can't bring new-fashion body for this life. Now people are very careful, particularly rich people from Arabia are saying, "I must go to make a checkup, because sometimes that sleeping not standing. I must go to make a checkup, to look at every organ, if working as before, particularly that one. And that one is dead one, finishing. No, we must make a checkup to make our physical being to be as before."

Finished! Don't run for checkup. Doctors making for you a quick *namar,* passing to cemetery. This virus does not differentiate between young or old ones. I must go and check if the pig flu has infected/reached me. If I did catch it, then I would ask to have like my bodyguard here. I must take bodyguard against pig flu. That virus, second one saying, "*Ya Hu*! You will be a foolish, idiot one. What are you saying? Doctors are not seeing the virus to be able to eradicate it. Don't make like this. People are learning, and yet the pig flu is running on them.

I am saying it is not so dangerous, but you must beware from dog flu. If dog flu coming to you, finishing you. Many people are going to pass away, because they are so lovely with dogs. If doctors say that you must kill dogs, some super-mind people would refuse to do so, saying, "If my dog is going to be killed, no." They would prefer their dogs to be taken away, rather than killing them. "I must be with my dog. Put me with my dog in same grave."

This is now a new fashion. New fashion people of the twenty-first century's civilization, are leaving Man and asking to live with animals. I am sorry to say that western civilization has just reached to that point. Yes, yes sir. They are so afraid; afraid of passing away. How passing away? They must take care. No matter how much they are taking care, death is reaching them, because their bodies will be melting, melting, melting and finishing.

O People! We are all surrounded by death everywhere, any time, in any condition, death is reaching us. You must care for a never-ending life. One that is never finishing. Eternity. Eternity; try to reach that grant from our Creator. He is granting us because we are giving our oath that, "We are Your servants." Those who will be His servants here, the Lord of Creation is going to grant them endless life, Eternal life. However, people have lost it. Now the whole world is running after something, but never understanding where they are going, what they are doing, and never asking to learn about their coming future. Yes, now perhaps seven billion people. I don't know if you can find 70,000 people who are really asking to reach Eternity.

O People! Give some time for your Lord to whom you gave your oath of servanthood when you said, "O our Lord! You are our Lord and we are your servants." Try to be His servants and not servant for your ego, *dunyā* or Shaytān. We are as all prophets were saying, warners. It is not an obligation to do so and for everyone to accept by force. No, you are free (to accept or reject). Use your good mind. Think on it and follow in the real direction that the Lord of Heavens is asking from you! He is inviting you, "Come to Me, O My Servants! Come to me!"

Unfortunately, they are not hearing that. They are hearing Shaytān, who is calling them from early morning up to late at night, to do this and that for him. They are wasting their chance; that chance is only granted once to us. There won't be another chance for us.

O People! *Ad-dīnu nasīha,* "Religion is advice." Prophet ﷺ was saying that religion means to ask goodness for people, and prevent them from falling into fire, here and in the Hereafter. May Allāh make us hear, learn and try to be our Lord's servants. May Allāh forgive us for the sake of the most honored one, Sayyidīna Muḥammad ﷺ!

May Allāh ﷻ forgive us.

Fātiḥah.

Run After Heavenly Ones

Aʿūdhu billāhi min ash-Shaytāni 'r-rajīm. Biṣmillāhi 'r-Raḥmāni 'r-Raḥīm. Dastūr, yā Sayyidī. Madad, yā rijālAllāh!

Dastūr yā Sayyidī, yā Sulṭān al-Awlīyā, madad! Aʿūdhu billāhi min ash-Shaytāni 'r-rajīm. Bismillāhi 'r-Raḥmāni 'r-Raḥīm. Lā hawla wa lā quwatta illa billāhi 'l-ʿAlīyyi 'l-ʿAdhīm! Allāhu Akbar, Allāhu Akbar, lā ilāha illa-Llāh, Allāhu Akbar, Allāhu Akbar, wa lillāhi 'l-ḥamd!

In Heavens there is one level where they are always saying, *Allāhu Akbar, Allāhu Akbar, lā ilāha illa-Llāh! Allāhu Akbar, Allāhu Akbar, wa lillāhi 'l-ḥamd!* That level of angels is never-ending; no one knows its beginning, no one knows its end. And we are giving our most high respect and glorification to our Lord that created us and granted us such an honor that no other creatures reached. And we are asking all prayings and all glory for Him, Almighty Allāh and we are asking that *alfu, alfu salāt, alfu, alfu salām.* No one knows beginning granted from Allāh Almighty to His most beloved one in His Divinely Presence. When beginning *as-salāt* and when ending, no beginning and no ending! Beginning from pre-Eternal ending up to Eternal (there is) Eternity, that no one knows beginning or ending for that! *Allāhu Akbar*! When granted to His most praised one in His Divinely Presence, Sayyidīna Muḥammad ﷺ.

O People! Hear, listen and obey. We are asking humbly from our master who is controlling and directing this planet; we are respecting him and asking that his heavenly holy powers reaching to us, (that we) be much more glorified ones in the Divine Presence. And we are saying *aʿūdhu billāhi min ash-Shaytāni 'r-rajīm,* to be in protection, to be sheltered under heavenly ones' powers. They have been granted such a power to look from ants to Man, and around Man are countless kinds of creatures. No one knowing the number of creatures, as well as no one knowing their positions. No one knows for what created, even they don't know, and as the deputies of our Lord we don't know about ourselves!

If the Lord of Heavens sending us holy ones and teaching us what is our mission, what is our beginning, and what is our targets, what is our final position? When you are saying "final," always new appearances from our Lord changing and according to divinely appearances, our position also changing. No creature going to be on same position from second-to-second or from third-to-third. That is very powerful position that no one knowing about, real positions, real targets, and real glorifying that they are doing day-by-day or hour-by-hour, minute-by-minute, second-by-second! You may go down and you can find a new creation with new appearances from their Lord. *Allāhu Akbar*!

Good tidings to those people who are running after such a magnificent appearances on themselves, or for everyone, whatever is going to be their missions through smallest part of time changing. That is Allāh's Holy Name, "al-Mubdi," and His Holy Name, "al-Khalaq," that countlessly creating from pre-Eternal running towards Eternal. What is pre-Eternal? and what is last Eternal? No one knows that between pre-Eternal and Eternal there is an appearance that we are asking Eternity, *azāli, abādi.*

Eternity: what is its space, what is its real being for, and what is it giving to Creation? Because never-ending grants coming from our Lord's endless treasures through endless territories, coming through dominions that have countless oceans and oceans! Each ocean, no one knowing its beginning or ending. And through that oceans' creatures, everyone has a mission for something created, and they are glorifying their Lord, Allāh Almighty, with another form of glorifying. And coming through those creatures *madad,* more than support. (It is) a divinely feeding, coming through every creature through Creation, and they are getting more lights. And each one's lights going to appear as lightening coming from Divinely Lights' Oceans; coming, touching to every creature, and appearing lightening so huge! And if that lightening coming as its real appearance (or) real power, this huge planet may burn, finishing! *Allāhu Akbar*! *Allāhu Akbar*! *SubḥānAllāh*!

They are granting now such things *Jabbar,* mighty, mighty appearances of the Lord, Allāh Almighty. If opening a little bit more with the very, very, very, very weakest application, this universe will disappear, coming through that ocean and finishing! Mankind, now they are getting much more proud. Therefore, coming such a *khitab,* addressing through heavenly ones, to make their pride down, down, down, until never going to be with Man any reason to be proud. They must know what we are saying! It is so big, so unlimited, to make people to be in Wondering Oceans or to be on astonishing level!

Therefore, when Divine Appearance comes to *ahlul-Jannah,* People of Paradise, they are seeing nothing there (because) nothing occupying there: no more beauty, no more taste after that looking. *Adhāmat,* Magnificent

Appearance (comes) on smallest time measure, and if *Adhāmat* finishes, a veil comes and this appearance returns to its original ocean. And when people are looking, they only see another paradise, another world, another Creation, because they can't look at anything except that weakest appearance, or the whole world is going to finish! So we must be happy, we must be so thankful to our Creator, that He created us in such an understanding level that no other creature may reach, not even angels!

People are losing their chance here for understanding such most simple things. It is also according to each planet, because this planet may be exposed a little bit more. Something on it just running through black hole and that black hole swallowing. White holes bringing new ones; just as a person is breathing, this space is breathing also, to show they are living ones. Not like you know if it is from fire or from rocks; that is what you are looking, and their real being is something else. Every time they are breathing, every time they are asking blessings from their Lord, everyone asking more and more lightening on them to be in existence.

People are playing by saying, "We are using rockets and reaching secrets of space." What is that? Ants laughing to them, because they are so idiot ones! No need to reach to that space that they are saying "billions of light years," but you can see and you may analyze something on a point. Here, that small one may be by holy command of Allāh Almighty like this universe, and you may see now it is like a map. But that (discovery) is to make people wake up and know something. As you are putting under a microscope and looking what is there, the whole (purpose is to make) people to look at the existence of the Lord of Heavens, and His dominions and His majestic oceans, to find that! May Allāh forgive us!

O People! Try to think on something that gives to you honor here and Hereafter, because such thinking is the key of secret treasures, and Allāh Almighty is preparing countless treasures for His deputies! Those treasures contain such valuable jewels, one of them going to be so much more valuable that if this planet is one piece of diamond, it is going behind that one like a zero! Allāh Almighty's treasures are countless, because when He is asking to grant to His servants something, only He may say, "Be (exist) for My servant!" and a different appearance coming into existence. Allāh Almighty says, "'Be!' And it will be (come into existence)."

O People! Think on it. You are getting powerful; you have been granted some point from Allāh Almighty, because you have an honor to be deputies, and that one from real value of sons of Adam will be granted by

Allāh Almighty! If this world is one thousand times that treasure, beyond that treasure is *Kun faya kun,* being granted from the sulṭān to His precious servants, all are not granted the same. That is our richness, not to have territories, not even to have continents, not even to have countless treasures; that has no value. The value you will be granted is from your Lord, Allāh Almighty!

Even one point of a small atom going to be bigger than all this Creation and just appearing a new being, new majestic planet that you did not see before and will not see after trying to reach such treasures. Is valuable lives for carcass? Don't waste your *dunyā* as a carcass! Run away from carcass people; run after such a beautiful beings and majestic glorified new planets, new territories for you! Why leaving that and running after carcass? You have mind? People now they lost their minds; factories or farms or whole countries are running after it, but (it has) no value. We are not using what granted to you, or (what) prepares you to be in the Divine Presence; that is valuable, so leave being dirty ones! Try to be clean ones, because those territories are only for clean ones and the Lord, Almighty Allāh, likes clean ones, those leaving *dunyā* to be heavenly ones. Dirty ones are those living on this planet. Leave dirtiness and run after clean ones and valuable ones.

O People! Come and listen! Don't lose such Eternal precious buildings, precious Creation. Run after it and leave what your ego asking, as it is dirty carcass of this life, but your real being, your spirituality is asking for highest positions and be in Eternity forever!

May Allāh forgive us and grant us some understanding. Don't fight with each other for a carcass. Think on it! All glory, all praising for Him, Almighty Allāh! Try to hear singing of angels, so beautiful, so tasteful.

May Allāh ﷻ forgive us.

Fātiḥah.

Be Family, Not Adversaries!

A'ūdhu billāhi min ash-Shaytāni 'r-rajīm. Biṣmillāhi 'r-Raḥmāni 'r-Raḥīm. Dastūr, yā Sayyidī. Madad, yā rijālAllāh!

Ant Allāh, anta Rabbuna, anta hasbuna, anta walīyuna, lā ilāha illa anta Subḥānak, Subḥānak, Subḥānak, SubḥānAllāhi 'l-'Adhīm wa bī ḥamdihi 'l-karīm, ighfir lana. Allāhu Akbar Allāhu Akbar, lā ilāha illa-Llāh Allāhu Akbar, Allāhu Akbar wa lillāhi 'l-ḥamd! Allāhu Akbar kabīra wa 'l-ḥamdulillāhi kathīra wa subhānAllāhi 'l-'Adhīm wa biḥamdihi 'l-karīm bukratan wa asīla lā ilāha illa-Llah, Allāhu Akbar, Allāhu Akbar wa lillāhi 'l-ḥamd!

We must be so happy, so proud, that our Creator granting us such an honor. No one knows its beginning and ending, and all is for the honor of the most praised and most glorified one in His Divine Presence, Sayyidīna Muḥammad ﷺ. Give more respect, take more blessings. *Alḥamdūlillāh,* that our Lord granting us to be from His most beloved one's nation. *Alḥamdūlillāh*! All thanks and glory is for our Lord, that He granted us such an honor.

O People! *As-salāmu 'alaykum wa raḥmatūllahi wa barakatuh*!

O the Seal of Prophets, *alfu, alfu salāt, alfu, alfu salām 'alayka wa 'alā ālika wa sahābatika, Yā khayra 'l-khalqi ajma'īn. Yā Rabbi zidhu, 'izzan wa sharafan, nūran wa masrūran, ridwānanwa ṣulṭāna.* He is *Sulṭān* and all Creation just is a grant to him. *SubḥānAllāh*!

And we are saying, *a'ūdhu billāhi min ash-Shaytāni 'r-rajīm. Bismillāhi 'r-Raḥmāni 'r-Raḥīm.* O our Lord, we are so weak. So weak creatures! Even in five minutes we will be tired of standing up, and it is not an excuse. We must stand up from beginning to end for His honor! O *ma'ashara 'n-nās*! O all Mankind! We are saluting you and saying, *As-salāmu 'alaykum,* such beautiful words from Heavens to Mankind, *As-salāmu 'alaykum*!

That *salām* from your Lord, from your Creator, Allāh, Jalla Jalaluhu, *as-salāmu 'alaykum. Raḥmatūllah* also, Allāh Almighty's mercy on you. It is such a big grant and honor that the Lord of Heavens is ordering, to be said among his deputies, *As-salāmu 'alaykum.* Say always for reaching such high levels. Going to be *salām* and *raḥmatūllah,* taking you up and up and up. Every time you are saying you are getting higher, higher, higher stations in heavenly levels and heavenly stations. Therefore, the Seal of Prophets was urging his nation to say to each other, *as-salāmu ʿalaykum wa raḥmatūllah.* Also another ocean of blessings and *wa barakātuh,* that is another ocean. That is a heavenly grant that we are using when we are giving salute to each other, *as-salām ʿalaykum wa raḥmatūllahi wa barakātuh*!

O People! Come and listen! We are using this as a beginning according to holy command of holy ones. When I am asking from our planets' master, that he is responsible for everything on this planet and he is that one who is bringing heavenly mercy and blessings on people, on living creatures. As well that bringing to botanic level; trees and plants, because plants also just created to give people, to make them happy. To make them pleased, to give them pleasure, to give them enjoyment, to give them heavenly wisdoms. Everything through existence is created for Mankind. The Lord of Heavens just decorating this huge planet with countless plants.

Once I was in Lebanon, touring to the big mountains, Urzu Lebnān, and we went to a heap. It was like a hill and it was protected by our Druze brothers. I am saying "brothers," some people may object on it. No, you can't do! Allāh Almighty created all Mankind to be brothers and sisters.

Lā tabāghadū, wa lā tadābarū, wa lā tahāsadū wa lā tadābarū wa kūnu ʿibādullāhi ikhwānan.

The Prophet ﷺ said, "Do not create hatred and do not envy and do not differ, and be altogether servants of Allāh as brothers."

Wa kūnu ihwānan. This is for all nations, Allāh Almighty's command, "O People! You must try to be brothers and sisters, the Lord of Heavens created you and gives everyone a specialty. Mankind is not created from a copy machine!

Wa jaʿalnākum shuʿūban wa qabā'ila li taʿarafū.

And We made you nations and tribes that Ye may know each other. 49:13

Allāh Almighty created Man and granted a specialty as a group of Mankind. Their out-looking and also their languages are different. Also, their manifestations getting different and their inner capacity or abilities different. You can't find two ones the same, because Allāh Almighty not making photocopy. No. When I am saying our 'Druze brothers,' yes, they are our bothers. Arabs, our brothers; Russians, our brothers; Chinese, our brothers; Americans, our brothers and Hungarians. We are saying that it is mentioned, 72 different groups of Mankind, and everyone just granted such a specialty. *SubḥānAllāh*! As our out-looking different, also our inner being, inner situation, manifestation, just different.

Yes, *li ta'arafū*. The Lord of Heavens is saying, "O People! I am granting to every nation and every group of people a specialty only for them, not for all." Arabs have a specialty and Turks another specialty. As our languages are different, our inner manifestations, our beings, are also different. Allāh Almighty is saying, *li ta'arafū*, "I created different tribes and nations for the *ummah* to know each other with their specialties." What is granted to English people is not granted to French people. What Germans are granted from their Lord's blessings is different from Russians, who have some specialty that Chinese people can't reach, and Japanese have such a specialty that Chinese people never reach.

Holy Qur'an is saying, *li ta'arafū;* you must observe and take wisdom from everyone as wisdoms open an understanding to your Creator. Without wisdoms, you are closed. Also saying, *li ta'arafū*, you must know each other. That one is Egyptian, that one is Lebanese, Iraqi, Turkish, Kurdish. Don't make yourself over others to say, "We are Turks and no one is reaching to our level," no! Kurdish people have been granted some specialties that Turkish people never reach. Like a crown on the head of a king or sulṭān; on that crown you can find countless jewels and each one is unique, never using another. Everyone is one, one, one. That is the perfection for that king. Allāh Almighty created Mankind and giving to everyone a special being. All of them going to be as a crown on the head of the Seal of Prophets, Sayyidīna Muḥammad ﷺ!

Don't make people down. You are saying, "We are highest nation," no! You have some specialty, Turks another specialty, Chinese another specialty and Kurdish another specialty. Don't make people *muhaqqar* (appear wretched.) Don't make people down. All of them on the same level, on same crown, but they have special places, special positions on that crown. You can't say diamond is the most valuable on crown and other jewels are no good. "I am the first, you are not good like me." It can't be. Allāh Almighty, He is the Creator and He created every nation and giving to them a specialty that no second one can carry.

Ruby is something else, pearl is something else, emerald is something else, diamond is something else, sapphire is something else. Jewels on a crown are not fighting each other, because they are looking; ruby looking at emerald and saying, "so beautiful." It is not saying, "I am much more beautiful than emerald." It has such a specialty that others are not carrying. There are some pearls, white ones, some pearls pink. Pink pearl is not saying, "I am better than this." White, carrying another specialty, beauty and benefit. Giving to people, to everyone, something else. It is for the benefit of Mankind.

All nations, *li ta'arafū*, meaning, "I created different nations and tribes and gave a specialty for each." So we must look at them, to know and take benefit from that ones' special wisdom or special being, something for us. But people are not understanding now, particularly Arabs; they know Arabic but instead of reciting *li ta'arafū,* they are understanding, *li tahārabū,* not to be together to give a beauty for Creation; instead they are fighting each other. This asking to destroy pearl; or diamond quarreling to destroy emerald and emerald running to destroy ruby. No! You must have a harmony. So beautiful, harmony, such that no one can think on it!

O our Listeners! Listen and try to understand what Holy Qur'an is saying. Can any book say in one holy verse such an end, showing people their life styles? It can't be. And people are following Shaytān, not following Holy Qur'an, saying arrogantly, "I am what I am!" Saying, our Druze brothers, yes, or Turkish brothers or Arab brothers or Jewish brothers, Russian brothers, Chinese brothers and sisters, Japanese people. There is a harmony that you can't imagine!

Therefore, I was ashaming to use some word against Creation and their foundations. Druze people, I am ashaming, because the Lord of Heavens just granted me such a specialty. Keep that specialty and give your *ihtirām,* respect to them. That is teaching of the Seal of Prophets ﷺ. Don't harm anyone with your hands or your tongue, or your power, by speaking or by acting. Who does these two things, it is not the honor of Mankind. Perhaps it is the specialty of animals. If you are going in front of animals, they may bite your hand. Anyone biting a second one, he and that animal are on the same level. Or if you are go behind an animal and it may be angry with you, these two legs kicking.

Who harms people with their tongues, he is not a real human being. Those giving trouble and harming people with their physical power are on the same level as animals. They are making me to speak this! I am not thinking something to say, but they are opening for the lowest level to teach our people, because now in this 21st Century all nations lost their levels for being deputies of the Lord of Heavens, falling under that level. That is the level of animals. Now people in such a way. Therefore, they are giving such teachings. We are not belonging to real human nature. We are falling down. We may stop here.

Once, as I said, we went on "Jabal Shaykh," Lebanon mountains and ante-Lebanon mountains. There was a hill protected by our Druze brothers, because some *mudīr*, harmful people, were harming the beauty on that hill and it was taken under protection. I was entering and they were taking some money from visitors, but they did not take anything from me, saying, "Welcome, O Shaykh!" They have such *adab*, respect. Then the guide said to me, "O Shaykh, there are one thousand different kinds of plants on this mountain."

What about in all east and west, north and south? How many thousands? Who is creating? And each one having a specialty. Nothing is created with *suda*, waste. If we are accepting and saying that each plant has a kind of specialty, what do you think about Mankind? Is our level under the level of plants? If Allāh Almighty grants to every plant a special wisdom, what about for Man? They were asking, saying, "Don't touch please, don't cut anything, don't step on it."

O our Listeners! What do you think? If the majestic command from Heavens orders, "O People! Keep well what I created, not to step on it and crush it," you must look and give your respect for its Creator. So the Creator of Man gave to everyone a specialty. We said for nations, if you are taking wider, we may say that everyone has a specialty. Therefore, stop killing, stop harming, stop giving trouble! Take away those terrible nuclear weapons! O Persians, O Russians, O Americans, O East and West people, leave that one. You are not giving life to people and you can't take their souls. Accept them for the honor of their Creator, and the Creator will accept you and grant to you.

May Allāh ﷻ forgive us.

Fātiḥah.

Renew Yourself for Your Lord

Aʿūdhu billāhi min ash-Shaytāni 'r-rajīm. Biṣmillāhi 'r-Raḥmāni 'r-Raḥīm.
Dastūr, yā Sayyidī. Madad, yā rijālAllāh!

A*stāghfirullāh. Dastūr yā Sayyidī, madad. As-salāmu ʿalaykum,* O our listeners. Don't listen to me, I know nothing, but you must try to hear, listen and obey the One who is granting us an understanding from His endless Mercy Oceans and asking us to be obedient servants. We may stand up for His glory and say, *Allāhu Akbar, Allāhu Akbar, lā ilāha illa-Llāh, Allāhu Akbar, Allāhu Akbar wa lillāhi 'l-ḥamd!*

We are giving our most high respects to that most honored one in His Divine Presence, Sayyidīna Muḥammad ﷺ. *Alfu salāt, alfu salām ʿalayka, yā Sayyidi 'l-Awwalīn wa 'l-Ākhirīn* (Master of the First and Last). You are *Nabī,* Prophet from pre-Eternal up to Eternal. All creations are giving you their salutes and most high respects. Please, *yā Sayyidi 'l-Awwalīn wa 'l-Ākhirīn,* O our most beloved *Rasūl,* give us from your intercession! That gives us honor here and Hereafter, forever.

O People! I am hearing and also you try to hear heavenly addressing to make you an honored one. Who is asking to be an honored servant must try to hear, listen and obey. That gives you an honor that is going to be more and more and never coming down and giving you honor forever. We are asking from our master, the master of this planet, *dunyā,* to look after us. We are asking the heavenly support of the grandmaster of this planet. There are so many masters on this planet, but only one is the most high and reaching to a heavenly level. He is the only one in the heavenly presence of the Seal of Prophets, Sayyidīna Muḥammad ﷺ.

We are saying, along with other people, *aʿūdhu billāhi min ash-Shaytāni 'r-rajīm.* All the time Shaytān is trying to harm Mankind and his mission is to give trouble to people. Those who listen to him are always falling in Trouble Oceans; always falling through oceans of miseries and suffering. We are saying, *aʿūdhu billāhi min ash-Shaytāni 'r-rajīm.* O our Lord, please give us Your protection, not to fall through Shaytān's traps; if they catch someone it is so difficult to save himself! Therefore, don't forget to say, *aʿūdhu billāhi min ash-Shaytāni 'r-rajīm,* to run away from Shaytān and *shaytanic* actings, efforts, and works.

What is the sign of *shaytanic* traps? First, Shaytān is showing you that it is a best being for Mankind and calling you, "Come here and you will be happy forever and find endless enjoyment." This is the first trap of Shaytān to catch people. Shaytān has countless traps, because there are now seven billion people. How many traps Shaytān is using? First Shaytān says, "O People! you must leave old things. You must "renew" your minds, your way of thinking. You must leave everything that you were doing."

"Therefore, O Mr. John, what do you think? New Year coming and bringing so many new things; so many new fashions, and you will look after new fashionable things. You must now change everything that you are using from clothes, eating, living, housewares; you must change your cars, your minds, and everything that belongs to Year 2009. You must *renew* yourselves." That is the first teaching. Therefore, you think, "Yes, a new year is coming and we must renew ourselves in every way of living, and every *sulūk, maslak*."

If you are going on this highway, you must change direction along another one, for example, "If you like to be free ones and become most understanding ones about your life ... you must change everything from the beginning up to end, from A to Z." In cars they have a book, A to Z. Shaytān is urging, "O People! First you must try to change your understanding (of) the way you look at everything, as new circumstances coming. You must try to arrange your lives in a different fashion."

O People! All those living on this planet; from small ones up to old ones, you are all thinking now and saying "a New Year," but it is really not going to be new; it is going to be old, not new. Why saying new? You must be happy like me, a person who is going to turn ninety this year. What happiness it brings me because I am now going to be a new one! Our lives on this planet going to be new. 2009 will become an old year, and 2010 the new year, which means we are also going to be new ones.

It is the worst *shaytanic* teaching for Mankind, that you are getting younger and younger! Every year whatever is new is going to be old, and when another year comes, it is a new year!

Apes can be cheated quickly and Shaytān is making people (to be) like apes, cheating them, saying, "You are getting 'renewing'; the New Year gives you a 'renewment'." First teaching of Shaytān for Mankind, cheating them, "You are getting younger. It is New Year, therefore, you must not use old-fashion things."

Everything inside, we may put outside, and we must bring new furniture, (then thinking,) "Oh, I am getting younger."

O People! Beware of Shaytān, cheating you in everything and making you not to think of dying and of death. Once upon a time your fathers and mothers were... (Mawlana coughs.) Shaytān is not happy with me, making me to not say what he is doing with people! They are thinking that a 'renewment' coming. They are never thinking that their last day is coming, because for everyone, there is a last day. There is no more life after that last day for them on this planet, and they will be taken by force or by surrendering.

Aʿūdhu billāhi min ash-Shaytāni 'r-rajīm, is a holy command from Heavens to all nations through every prophet. It was sent as a warning, "O People! Don't listen to Shaytān, it is cheating you and you will regret it."

Aʿūdhu billāhi min ash-Shaytāni 'r-rajīm. You must beware of Shaytān, its orders and ideas; they may change every year, but they bring the same point that takes Man into darkness. Shaytān's thinking and main point is to take people from enlightened worlds to dark worlds. As mentioned through heavenly knowledge in holy books, the Lord of Heavens sent every prophet as a warner. All prophets were warners bringing 124,000 reminders to all Mankind, because biggest harm coming to people from *shaytanic* cheating.

O People! Now after fifteen days a new year is coming. Don't be cheated! Look at what your Creator, the Lord of Heavens, is saying and what He is asking from you: to be new always for His heavenly service.

O my listeners! Don't listen to me but listen to His holy and heavenly messages through prophets. What He is saying, "O My servants, don't forget that you are My servants, and I am asking best servanthood from you. O My servants, you are refusing to be My servants and occupying yourselves with nonsense through this life. What is that 'renewment'? How you are asking 'renewment' when you see daily, thousands, millions of people running away from this life to other, unknown territories? Why are you not thinking on it?

O my listeners! Make your ego believe in holy commands of the Lord of Heavens, and follow these commands: you will be honored. As long as you are hearing and obeying Shaytān, you are losing your honor and you will be dishonored. As long as you are trying to follow His heavenly services, you will reach a position that gives you honor over honor, life over life, lights over lights, happiness on happiness. You will find the best from everything! That is the honor of being from Mankind. The Lord of Heavens granting them that honor, because He is saying, "You are My servants. I am accepting you to be My servants through My heavenly levels, through My Heavens."

People now are only hearing and asking to follow the *shaytanic* teachings that are coming through PhD people, doctors and professors. All of them first in line, listening to Shaytān, saying, "You are true." If someone is saying to them, "Listen to what the Lord of Heavens is saying," they are never happy, instead when hearing Shaytān and *shaytanic* nonsense and dirty things, they are very happy!

The holy command from Allāh Almighty is, "Don't eat dirty things! O People! You are created clean and I am granting to you clean foods for your physical being. Keep my enjoyful grants, it is for your honor. I am forbidding you to eat and drink dirty things, because only pigs eating dirtiness, even their dirt they are eating. Don't eat pigs, because they are dirty."

The Lord of Heavens is saying to human nature, "I am creating you clean and offering you clean things and I am ordering you to use clean things. Don't eat and drink dirty things. I made for you clean food and clean drinks. If you are not listening to Me and eating and drinking dirty things, you are losing your heavenly appearance on the Day of Resurrection and are coming like dogs and pigs, that are eating their dirtiness also." You will come like this, but where are people, (are they) ever hearing or listening or asking to keep that order? When they pass away, they will find themselves through dirty sewage channels saying, "What is that?!!" That is what you were eating through your life: sleep in it, eat and drink it. Allāh ﷻ protects us!

O People! Use your minds and try to hear, to listen and to obey your Lord's holy commands. You will be best ones in the Divine Presence! You will be rewarded such grants that no one before is seeing, hearing or knowing! Be patient. Be patient against your egos, be patient against the demands of Shaytān and you will be happy here and Hereafter.

This is well-known knowledge. People just caught through *shaytanic* tricks and traps that are ready and you can find them everywhere. Tricks that are catching people and putting through traps. (Shaytān says,) "Be free ones!" Everywhere people are saying, "We need freedom." Freedom for what? Real freedom is to be free from Shaytān and from your ego and its demands. Leave them, so that you will be (truly) free ones! If not, 'freedom' has no meaning and you are being ridden by Shaytān, like a Man riding his donkey. Shaytān is riding on you and sending you everywhere that is not clean, but dirty.

Think on it! This is an important warning for everyone nowadays, because a year has passed that was full of troubles, miseries, and sufferings. As they are saying, the coming year would be a new period of time, one new year. Beware, and keep yourself from falling through oceans of troubles and miseries in the coming year. Don't just prepare yourself for one night or one day, dressing in beautiful clothes and having so many foods, eating dancing and singing. That is not for you! What your Lord is asking for you is to be clean ones and prepare yourselves. A day will come, your last day, when you will be taken from this life to another unknown distance. May Allāh ﷻ forgive us.

O People! *Ad-dīna 'n-nasīhat*, "Religion is advice." All prophets did this as much as they could, but people never liked their advice and went against them, killing them or sending them away. Finally, heavenly punishment and cursing came on them, finishing them and making them disappear. May Allāh protect us!

Give time for your Lord's advice. Hear heavenly advising and try to be even a weak servant. We are weak servants, (but) try to keep it. At least if we can't keep servanthood fully, we must try as much as possible to do something; everything that would make our Lord pleased with us. If you are pleasing your Lord, He will make you pleased also. If you make everything for the sake of pleasing the Divine Presence, the Lord of Heavens would make you to be joyful, here and Hereafter.

We are asking for forgiveness from Allāh Almighty for the most honored one, Sayyidīna Muḥammad ﷺ, *yā Rabbī*. May Allāh ﷻ forgive us. This is a warning for all Mankind before cursing is coming. Protect yourself!

May Allāh ﷻ forgive us.

Fātiḥah.

The Worldly Versus Heavenly Show

Aʿūdhu billāhi min ash-Shaytāni 'r-rajīm. Biṣmillāhi 'r-Raḥmāni 'r-Raḥīm. Dastūr, yā Sayyidī. Madad, yā rijālAllāh!

Dastūr yā Sayyidī, madad. Allāhu Akbar, Allāhu Akbar, lā ilāha illa-Llāh, Allāhu Akbar, Allāhu Akbar, wa lillāhi 'l-ḥamd! Alfu, alfu salāt, alfu, alfu salām. Countless salutes, honors and glory to you, O our most beloved Prophet! The most beloved and honored one in the Divine Presence, Sayyidīna Muḥammad ﷺ.

As-salāmu ʿalaykum, O our Listeners! May Allāh bless you. May Allāh ﷻ forgive us. And, O our master, master of this world that we are on, salutes to you and respect to you also. We are asking your holy authority to make an arrangement on this planet, to be a beloved planet in heavenly levels.

O People! All of us know nothing. But we must try to know, to learn, and to understand, something. We must try to know about ourselves. We are need to know and understand what we are knowing. Without understanding, knowing giving nothing to people. Therefore, understanding is the most important point through our lives. We must try to understand. If we are not trying to understand something, then our levels will be on level of the world of animals.

That is a pity for a person who has been granted to be a king, a majestic king. Leaving that and asking to come to level of animals. That is a grant from Allāh Almighty. Pity! If we are losing a chance that we have been granted and asking to run on level of animals. Why? You are a mad one? No balance for you? To know and to understand? Which one from Mankind is asking not to continue on the level of Mankind? Who is going to say, "I don't like that and I prefer to be on the level of animals?" Now we are in it; our situation now on this planet is on the same line. People are saying, "We are never interested in heavenly things. Give us what you are giving to animals, that is, to enjoy ourselves. Why you are asking us to be on unknown levels?" That is their understanding for their lives on this planet.

O People! Say, *aʿūdhu billāhi min ash-Shaytāni 'r-rajīm.* Don't forget it because Shaytān is cheating you and carrying you from your real, honorable level to the level of animals; even under that level. It is a pity.

O People! Say, *aʿūdhu billāhi min ash-Shaytāni 'r-rajīm*. O our master, we are running to you, not to be cheated with Shaytān calling us. Please keep ourselves. We are running under your protection. Please protect ourselves not to fall through the trips of Shaytān. But people now are thinking something else. So many things we must try to learn. Say, *Bismillāhi 'r-Raḥmāni 'r-Raḥīm*. By the name of That One who created us. For the honor of the most honorable one in the Divine Presence, ask, what we have been granted. To reach and to keep that honor. The level of animals is a blame for you.

O Mankind! You are so proud that we are reaching 2010. You may reach 2000 or 3000 or more, but if you are not changing your reality, that grant from Allāh Almighty to you, not changing yourselves to reach that level, then there is no value for you. Think on it.

O People! Say, *Bismillāhi 'r-Raḥmāni 'r-Raḥīm*. That is our sword for fighting against Shaytān and its armies. You may ask, where are the armies of Shaytān? He has volunteers. Without payment, Shaytān may call thousands and millions to be his volunteers.

In this world now, there are perhaps seven billion people from Mankind who have been created and honored by their Creator. But people are leaving that saying, "No, we don't like this. We must run after Shaytān. We must try to reach what Shaytān is promising us. We must run after that one. We are not asking to run towards our Lord's heavenly levels." Why? Use your mind! Today you are here, tomorrow you can be through graveyard. What happened? What you are taking? What is your profit? Give something, and take all things.

That is the mentality for clever ones. Clever ones always using a balance, but their balance is not the balance of this world. Asking for heavenly balance and their Lord promising and granting it to His deputies and servants; to take heavenly balance and use it. That heavenly balance is never getting to be wrong, but the balance that you are using through this life, may be from beginning up to end, showing you wrong ways. Wrong on wrong.

SubḥānAllāh, glory to Allāh Almighty! But people just changed and asking daily a new changing for themselves. They like to be seen everyday with another suit in another show. People like show and the biggest trip of Shaytān, insisting to people, saying, "O People! you must make show daily. Everyday you must be seen in another show." That is what they like, their last limit. Mankind likes show. Is it not so, my listeners? At least you like to make a show with your dog. So many kinds of dogs and there is a very ugly one, what is its name? Churchill? You can't look at that one. Like this, strange. I am saying to people, from where bringing this show with dogs? They like to carry everyday at least one kind of dog to make a show.

O People! Don't run to make a show with yourself or your animals for other people. You must try to make a show for Heavens, so that day-by-day your face is getting much more bright. That is a show, not with your cats or dogs, or with your cars or your clothes. From where is this shirt? What written? 'Marks & Spencer.' Countless people entering and countless getting out and taking something to be a show for them. For ladies, that they like always to be seen beautiful, it doesn't matter. But you as a man, running after show, for what is that show? The Lord of Heavens created you for show?

If you are doing a show, make your show for heavenly ones, not Mankind. You and me and he and she, we are all on the same level. Why you are trying to make a show to you or you to me, for what? But Shaytān saying, "Oh, people most important thing that you must do for being an important one, you must do a 'show.'" Therefore, first, who likes show? Soldiers. They are very proud making their 'shows.' They are saying, "Anyone like ourselves, with white gloves"? And no moustache, no beard, and there is a sword, also epaulets on their shoulders. No one likes a show like soldiers. They think they are the lords of Earth!

All of you like pariah, lowest level in India. Conservative people also like show and coming secondly, Labor Party members. Why you are forgetting? Why are you saying this? It is no good to say 'Labor.' It is a shame on you. Wearing suits and saying, "We are Labor Party people," never making it true. When you are coming to parliament, you must do your show to make a difference between Conservatives and Labor. You must bring a shovel, hammer, ropes and big shoes. In such a way you must do your show as a laborer. Why are you dressing and coming to parliament and saying, "We are Labor Party people?" No good show. That is a very dirty show. You must dress to show people that you are something!

For what Shaytān urging people to make show? Because people mostly are idiot ones. Who are the idiot ones? Those people who are not using their mentality. Mentality never saying to you to use something to make a show or that you are something. But Shaytān is blowing through their dirty egos, making people run after a show; they live and work for show. That is the main target people are running after in our days.

After one week will be 2010. Every time they are trying to make a show. When they are getting out, when riding on a horse, when riding on don..."Don't say, O Shaykh, donkey." How they make show, doesn't matter. Like me, I may ride on a donkey. My show is donkey, doesn't matter. But you are asking for a horse to make a show. "Now it is not time of horse, O Shaykh." Yes I know, but you like it, therefore, you may try to have a car, for car show. Who is sitting in, such a princess or Mercedes or another, Rolls Royce people.

People make a scenario. I may also do with them, to be seen that I am making a show. "Who is your teacher?" No one is my teacher, but I may think on it, I am looking sometimes, seeing good, but sometimes I am seeing something upside down. I am making a show. Sometimes I am making a show also to Shaykh Hisham because he is saying to me, "O Shaykh, put wax here also (Mawlana curls his moustache) and it will become a very good show for you."

Our *suhbah,* association, tonight is very important, O my listeners! Don't laugh. You are also like me. Everyone likes to make a show and the whole world, from small ones up to old ones, are running after shows to make people interested with them. They will be happy when people are looking and saying, "What a stylish person, although he is 90-years-old but so elegant." That is enough for me that people looking to me and saying, "What an elegant person." He is not thinking that people say, "He just lost his mind and became like an ape!"

Our master is teaching now, from east to west, even through Africans, through Tibetan people, through Indian people, to show themselves with a new show. For this reason governments are making wars and fighting. People are running in streets and saying, "We are democratic people," others saying, "No, we are socialist people," others saying, "We are Tibetan Buddhist. Much more heavenly people on Earth, look ourselves, we are making 'show.'" Small ones, big ones, women, and men, they are doing this.

People are losing their ways and this is an important point. No one is asking to make a show for themselves when they are passing from this life to the real life. It is mentioned through all holy books that when a person passing, dying, his or her soul is going up with angels towards Heavens. And some people are saying, "So beautiful one, so enlightened one, so elegant one." And for others, "O so dirty ones, so ugly one, so idiot one, so dark one." They are not thinking on it, that on the Last Day their soul is going to be taken to Heavens, therefore, try to make show there so that angels will say, "So beautiful, so elegant, so enlightened servant of our Lord. Welcome to you." They are not thinking that. For those no-mind people who are trying to make 'shows' on this planet, when coming up, going to be in ugliest show, ugliest one! Angels saying, "So dirty, so hated one, so ugly one," and running away.

O People! One day is coming that you will be finishing your life here and angels taking you up and the angels of Heavens will look to you. Make your show there, the real show, with heavenly lights. Try to be enlightened ones so that angels will say, "So beautiful, so elegant, so perfect one." Do your show there, not here, no. If you are trying to make show on this planet, your level under level of animals because no animal asking to make show. At least they are keeping their origins and they are happy, never trying to make a 'show.'

O People! Listen and obey. Ask from your Lord that beautiful show. Don't ask from Shaytān to say to you, "O you are so beautiful," no. May Allāh ﷻ forgive us. That is our trying from Allāh Almighty. O People! use your minds! You can reach highest levels of humanity. If not, you may fall down under level of animals. *Astaghfirullāh.* We are asking for forgiveness from our Lord and asking His blessings for the honor of the most honored one in His Divine Presence, Sayyidīna Muḥammad ﷺ.

Don't do anything for show. Who making everything for show, that one and Shaytān on the same level. But try to do everything for your Lord's pleasement, enjoyment and pleasure. That is the honor that we are gaining. Try to reach the heavenly show, not on Earth.

Yā Rabbī, yā Rabbī, yā Rabbī. From one word, one whole association comes, signifying that with one word you are playing and that is making you either to fall down or to be taken up: "show." Good show and bad show. *Astaghfirullāh.*

May Allāh ﷻ forgive us.

Fātiḥah.

Those Who Say There Is No God

A'ūdhu billāhi min ash-Shaytāni 'r-rajīm. Bismillāhi 'r-Raḥmāni 'r-Raḥīm. Dastūr, yā Sayyidī. Madad, yā rijālAllāh!

Dastūr yā Sayyidī, madad yā Rasūlullāh! Stand up for our Lord, for our Creator! All praisings and all glory is for our Lord, Allāh Almighty, from pre-Eternal up to Eternal! O People! Try to be in the Divine Presence, as much as you can do from praisings and glory to be happy here and Hereafter. *Allāhu Akbar, Allāhu Akbar, lā ilāha illa-Llāh, Allāhu Akbar, Allāhu Akbar, wa lillāhi 'l-ḥamd! Allāhu Akbar khabīra, w'alḥamdūlillāhi kathīra, wa SubḥānAllāhi bukratan wa 'asīla, lā ilāha illa-Llāh, wa wahdahu lā sharīk lah, yuhiyy wa yumīt wa huwa 'alā kulli shay'in qadīr. Subḥānsen yā Rabb ṣulṭānsen yā Rabb mutlaq ṣulṭān sensin.*

And we are asking humbly from Your Divine Presence to be granted to our most beloved Prophet, our Messenger Rasūlullāh, to grant him more and more from Your Glory and Praising. After Allāh ﷻ, who is that one to whom we may grant our endless glorifying and honoring and praising, is only Sayyidīna Muḥammad ﷺ!

As salāmu 'alaykum, O our Listeners! O human nature, hear and listen, listen and obey, come and listen, don't escape, what you can like take it, if you don't like it leave it. This is such a big market—not flea market, flea market for me (laughter)—but for you, you are asking something more because you like to make show. Therefore, you are looking for everything to be the best one, but I am a weak, poor dervish, looking what from Heavens runs on Mankind freely. Likes may fade away; I am going to carry them to collect.

O People! Try to collect what will be for you forever! Don't run after something imitations, of no value. They may exist continuously up to the Day of Resurrection, and after it finish. *A'ūdhu billāhi min ash-Shaytāni 'r-rajīm.* Run away from Shaytān and try to be good ones; if you are bad ones you will be punished.

Allāh ﷻ may ask, "O My servant! Did you do your best, or not? O My servant! You did your worst or nothing? O My servant! Did you bring the good things granted to you by your Lord? What you did with them? Did you send them to Me or to *shaytanic* ways? What you did, say to Me! I grant to you so many things, everything to be under your command, under your demand, under your wishing, under your will! What you did? Did you use them in a best way and sending them to My Divine Presence, or not?"

When the Lord of Heavens is angry, divine anger will come and people begin to tremble, even prophets and messengers fall on their knees for the *haybat*, His divine anger!

O People! That day is coming. Think on it! Send to your heavenly level what you will have there, that is granted to you. Send from now for that Day, to be for you forever like a paradise. Send that first. The Lord of Heavens will ask, "O My servant! Tell me, what did you send to My Divine Presence? Do you think I created you like animals, to not think, or that I did My best for you? Of all Creation, I did My best to you, O My servant! Did you do your best for Me? Are you sending me your best? Say to me! I did My best for you, but you are not doing your best for Me! Take this one to be with Shaytān!"

Yes, it is enough if Allāh Almighty is saying, "O My servant! On the Day of Resurrection, the same questioning," (or) saying to you, "O My servant! Enough, no need for any other question." Think on it! If your Creator asks you, "O My servant! I did My best to you! Do you think I did My worst to you? What are you thinking? I did My best to you, but do you think that you did your best for Me?"

That is the question! O pope, say to your followers! O chief rabbi, warn your people! O Muslim world that they're trying to be non-Muslims, running after western countries everywhere, and Muslim countries' people are saying, "We are asking to be westernized people." *Ptuu* (spit) on you! Who is asking to be westernized people and Allāh granting to you highest honor, and you are saying, "We are leaving this and getting to be westernized people," what is their honor in the Divine Presence? If you will be a westernized people, what is your honor, what is your value in the Divine Presence? O pope, O patriarchies, O chief rabbis, all rabbis, all bishops, and particularly those Muslim *ʿulama*! I am shouting to them, they're not opening their mouth to say, "We are Muslims, and we are only asking our Lord's pleasure with us, and His pleasure is only when we are following His holy orders!"

Where is Muslim *ʿulama*? Where is Salafi *ʿulama*? Where is Wahabi people (leaders)? Where is Afghani leaders? Where is Pakistan leaders? Where is Turkish *ʿulama*? Why you are not warning your people? Allāh likes us to be His servants, not democrats or capitalist or socialist or Shaytānist?

Say! Coming some days now, after a few weeks coming something that going to be beginning of Armageddon! That means:

Inna batsha rabbika la-shadīd.

Verily, thy Sustainer's grip is exceedingly strong! *85:22*

Your Lord's anger coming on people; first on Muslim ones whom asking to be westernized people. They are leaving everything from Islam and bringing everything from non-Muslims or westernized people. We are not accepting! We are not accepting! Hah! Keep what we are saying now, O Muslims listeners, and also all Mankind. What Allāh Almighty calling you and will ask to you, "O My servant! do you think that I did My best for you?" What it will be your answer to your Lord, for your Creator?! Are you not ashaming to say, "We are saying there is no god! We are atheists!"

What is that? O Muslim World, for what you will be 70 and more branches according to a *ḥadīth* of Sayyidīna Muḥammad ﷺ, "My nation will leave my way and they will be in 73 groups. The Lord of Heavens is sending His holy orders through me, and from my way only one group will be on the right way."

When Allāh Almighty will ask them, "Do you think that I did for you My best?" only one from 73 branches will answer, 'Yes,' because all others left that real way that the Seal of Prophets ﷺ has been ordered to declare to all nations! Do you think that he was mentioning that one who will be acceptable? Paradise people—do you ink that they will be democratic people or liberal people or socialist people or communist people or Marxist people or ape-ist... there is ape-ist also? (laughter)

O Shaykh, there is new news, that people running after pig flu! They are occupied with pig flu and asking how to save themselves from pig flu. And one philosopher is saying, "O People! Try to be pigs, then you will be in safety because that virus is knowing that you are pigs and never touching to you, no need for vaccination!"

O our Listeners! Don't listen to Shaytān! Shaytān is saying, "Be like pigs, you will be in safety!" Therefore, heavenly anger is approaching, like when Nimrod was waiting to fight the armies of Heavens, and he asked Sayyidīna 'Ibrahim ﷺ, "Where are the armies of your Lord? I am here!"

Sayyidīna 'Ibrahim ﷺ said, "Be patient a little…look, now they are coming."

"Where?" Then just appeared from horizon a small black shape, like small black clouds.

Sayyidīna ʿIbrahim ﷺ said, "My Lord's armies approach, so beware, and keep yourself!"

Nimrod was trembling and didn't know what to do, looking, looking and surprising! (He was thinking,) "How is that armies of your Lord?" and after a while he asked again, "Where are these armies of your Lord?"

And when he looked, beginning sounds coming from the horizon, "*Huuuuuuuuuuuuuuuuuuuuuu*," louder and louder, then arriving to Nimrod. First the sound was "*Hu hu hu hu hu hu hu hu hu hu hu*," making their nervous system finish! Then a trembling came on his soldiers dressed in iron armors with their swords and arrows. Then came this sound, "*Hu hu hu hu hu hu hu hu hu hu hu*," filling everywhere and they fell down without that reaching them!

O People! I am a weak servant, but the Lord of Heavens can come to my ear with the sound of Armageddon; that will take six of seven people, only one remains and six taken away.

wa mā dhālika ʿalā Allāhi bi-ʿazīz.

And for Allāh that is not at all difficult. 14:20

O *ʿulama* al-Azhar, O *ʿulama* Hijāz, O *ʿulama* Madinah al-Munawwara, O Iraqi people, don't make explosions! Be quiet! Prepare yourself and try to make *tawbah*, repent to our Lord!

O Pope! Your Christian nations are inventing so many terrible weapons, and warn them don't do that!

O People! The Lord of Heavens never created you to be worst ones to each other, but He ordered you to be best ones! Is it true? I am a weak servant; I am nothing and I am shouting! You must hear, you must listen, you must obey or coming Armageddon worse than you can ever imagine!

O People! Don't think that I am shouting to you, no; to my ego, to my *nafs* I am shouting and warning, and everyone may warn their egos because egos are always with Shaytān; Shaytān is always against the Lord's heavenly orders. Try what they are making me to say on this holy night, that from your Lord it is written in the Old Testament, New Testament, Psalms and Holy Qur'an, that all prophets have been granted heavenly orders written for them, and everyone knows that Allāh Almighty will ask you:

If there is nothing else in all religions, only this enough! Try to know from religions, from holy books, try to learn and follow that command.

"O My servant! Do you think you did your best for Me?" My listeners, where you are escaping you must listen to this or heavenly anger that is approaching will take away six people from seven! You know! You know! You know! You know!

O Muslims! You are never going to be saved in the Divine Presence when He asks you, "Do you think you did your best for me?" and you are saying, "O our Lord! We were making high buildings, skyscrapers, and we did everything that western people did and much more than them."

O *ʿulama*! Where is your advice to your people? All Muslims! Stop killing and try to prepare an answer for when Allāh Almighty will ask you, "O My servant! I did for you My best. Did you do your best for Me?" There is no benefit from any book if you cannot say, "O My Lord! I tried to make my best for You!" If you did not learn this, your life will be *suda*, wasted!

O People! This is a holy night and holy anger is approaching and making me such a volcano, and I am so fearing from Allāh Almighty's blaming! O our Lord, forgive us, forgive us, forgive us! My days and your days are going to finish. I am shouting and warning all people. No one can say against our words granted to speak to you tonight.

Finished! Write this down and learn it, or a heavenly whip is approaching and Armageddon will open its doors.

Tawbah yā Rabbī, tawbah yā Rabbī, tawbah astaghfirullāh, tawbah astaghfirullāh! For the honor of Your best one, forgive us and send us who can keep us, your weak servants, on Your brightened way!

May Allāh ﷻ forgive us.

Fātiḥah.

Say, Bismillahi 'r-Rahmani 'r-Rahim!

Aʿūdhu billāhi min ash-Shaytāni 'r-rajīm. Biṣmillāhi 'r-Raḥmāni 'r-Raḥīm. Dastūr, yā Sayyidī. Madad, yā rijālAllāh!

Allāhu Akbar, Allāhu Akbar, lā ilāha illa-Llāh, Allāhu Akbar, Allāhu Akbar, wa lillāhi 'l-ḥamd! Allāhu Akbar, Allāhu Akbar, lā ilāha illa-Llāh, Allāhu Akbar, Allāhu Akbar, wa lillāhi 'l-ḥamd! Allāhuma salli wa sallam wa bārik ʿalā Sayyidīna Muḥammad!

O People! Say, *aʿūdhu billāhi min ash-Shaytāni 'r-rajīm. Bismillāhi 'r-Raḥmāni 'r-Raḥīm.* Whoever is asking protection, must say, *aʿūdhu billāhi min ash-Shaytāni 'r-rajīm.* All evil and devils belong to Shaytān, their teacher, who is always disobedient to Allāh Almighty. And say, *Bismillāhi 'r-Raḥmāni 'r-Raḥīm.* That is our sword, on our egos and *shaytans,* on the necks of devils.

O our Grandshaykh ق, master of this planet! We are asking for your heavenly powers to reach your people for whom you are responsible in the heavenly presence of the Seal of Prophets ﷺ.

O People! Always say, *aʿūdhu billāhi min ash-Shaytāni 'r-rajīm* and, *Bismillāhi 'r-Raḥmāni 'r-Raḥīm.* That is our protection here and Hereafter! Whoever is forgetting to say, *Bismillāhi 'r-Raḥmāni 'r-Raḥīm,* he has been forgotten in the heavenly levels. His name will be never written that he may enter, or that he may reach to Heavens. If anyone is not saying, *Bismillāhi 'r-Raḥmāni 'r-Raḥīm,* it is impossible to reach their heavenly levels. It is important. Now people have forgotten it! People, particularly the Muslim world have lost their chance through heavenly powers, which reaches them by saying, *Bismillāhi 'r-Raḥmāni 'r-Raḥīm.*

O our Listeners from east to west, from north to south! Hear and obey. Try to be obedient servants. Look at the many statesmen; do you think any one of them says, *Bismillāhi 'r-Raḥmāni 'r-Raḥīm* when they address to people? Wake up! Blame on them, they are saying they are presidents, prime ministers, kings, *sulṭāns, amīrs.* I never heard, perhaps some of them say it. But mostly I never heard them say, *Bismillāhi 'r-Raḥmāni 'r-Raḥīm* when they address to people. You must say it! If you are not saying it, you are not going to be protected or sheltered (from) Armageddon. Armageddon is at the door.

Don't fear from pig flu as that is nothing. But something is coming which is mentioned in every prophets' declaration; before the Last Day is coming, before the Day of Resurrection, there will be the Greatest War (Armageddon) that never happened before. So many people will pass away and from all the horrible destruction, nothing will remain of them but dust. Yet our Muslims states are not trying to say *(dhikr), Bismillāhi 'r-Raḥmāni 'r-Raḥīm, Bismillāhi 'r-Raḥmāni 'r-Raḥīm, Bismillāhi 'r-Raḥmāni 'r-Raḥīm, Bismillāhi 'r-Raḥmāni 'r-Raḥīm, Bismillāhi 'r-Raḥmāni 'r-Raḥīm, Bismillāhi 'r-Raḥmāni 'r-Raḥīm, Bismillāhi 'r-Raḥmāni 'r-Raḥīm*!

You could walk from east to west, and the Muslim *ummah* was running like rivers from unknown deserts towards east and west, saying *(dhikr), Bismillāhi 'r-Raḥmāni 'r-Raḥīm, Bismillāhi 'r-Raḥmāni 'r-Raḥīm, Bismillāhi 'r-Raḥmāni 'r-Raḥīm, Bismillāhi 'r-Raḥmāni 'r-Raḥīm, Bismillāhi 'r-Raḥmāni 'r-Raḥīm, Bismillāhi 'r-Raḥmāni 'r-Raḥīm, Bismillāhi 'r-Raḥmāni 'r-Raḥīm*! And angels were coming. When those *mushriks,* idol-worshippers, came against Islam and Muslims were saying together with Prophet ﷺ, reciting, *Bismillāhi 'r-Raḥmāni 'r-Raḥīm*! Allāh Almighty sent to Arabs, they know *āyatu 'l-karīmah*:

> *Yumdidkum rabbukum bi-khamsati ālāfin mina 'l-malā'ikati musawwimīn.*
>
> *Yea, if you remain firm and act aright, even if the enemy will rush here on you in hot haste, your Lord would help you with five thousand angels wearing turbans with tails."* *Ali-'Imrān, 3:125*

And when Rasūlullāh ﷺ looked that the angels were coming on horses and *musawwimīn*, the end of turban of Prophet ﷺ was like this, and he was saying *āyatu 'l-karīmah.* Arabs know this, but they are not using and putting some cloth over their heads. It is not good for them. They must keep the *sunnah,* the ways of the Seal of Prophets ﷺ. Yes, they are not using this. If they are seeing this, they are getting very angry. Thousands blames on them, who refuse to use this turban. They should repent!

This is a protection. If fire is running from Heavens, who are wearing turbans on their heads, it can't touch them. And women whose heads are covered, veiled, who keep themselves with heads covered, nothing will ever touch them. Holy orders of Heavens, you must take care. If not, you will suffer!

Yes, all people must come to what the Seal of Prophets ﷺ, Sayyidīna Muḥammad ﷺ, is calling them. I am only a weak warner to you! Keep yourselves. Don't be ashamed for those people who are leaving the heavenly orders and heavenly appearances, because this appearance for *mu'mins* is heavenly. Angels are on such a way. Yes. *Allāhu Akbar, Allāhu Akbar*!

O our Lord! Don't leave us to our bad egos. Bad egos are following Shaytān. And don't be like Shaytān, whom Allāh Almighty ordered angels to make *sajdah* to Adam. Salafi people say kissing hands is *harām*, but what about *sajdah*? They are Arabs reciting Holy Qur'an and looking that Allāh Almighty ordered to make *sajdah* to Adam, but they are so clever and learned. If a person is kissing some one's hands, they are saying, *mushrik, mushrik* (idol-worshipper)!! They are *mushriks*! How?

O Salafi and Wahabi *ʿulama*! O PhD doctors! You are so proud, saying you can't kiss hands. You don't clean under yourself? Then come and teach to me. I may teach you and from east to west. They are not using water for their *taharah* (in bathroom); they are using toilet paper, saying, "We can't touch." Let Shaytān touch you!

Angels are not writing this for me on my left side. I may say good things and they are writing, but if I say bad things, they are not writing. He is retired (more than 80 years old)! (laughter) I am speaking truth! What are you saying? Yes, Allāh Almighty ordered all angels to make *sajdah* and all are making *sajdah*; only Shaytān said, "I am not making *sajdah,* I am not obeying." (Mawlana laughs.) Arabs will be very angry. Yes, yes. And look at Shaytān's custom. Shaytān is saying, "I am never making *sajdah* for Adam!"

Once every 100,000 years he is brought and Allāh Almighty is ordering the angels to bring out Shaytān out of hells and to bring here. The angels are bringing and the Lord of Heavens by angels is ordering to tell him and calling Adam ﷺ from inside and saying, "O Iblīs! Make *sajdah* and enter Paradise." He is saying, "I am never making *sajdah* for Adam, no, no, no!" Take him back to fire; that is Shaytān's *tabiyyat,* custom. Therefore, don't be like Shaytān, saying, "We are never leaving new-fashion life, not leaving westernized life, not coming back to Islam!" Don't follow Shaytān! Look at the holy command of Allāh Almighty.

O People! You will be happy forever; Eternal life awaits you! *Astaghfirullāh, astaghfirullāh, astaghfirullāh, tawbah yā Rabbī, tawbah yā Rabbī.* We are asking as our most honored Prophet ﷺ was saying, "O our Lord! Don't leave us in the hands of our bad egos." I am only saying this and I am asking protection. Protection is our sword, to say, *aʿūdhu billāhi min ash-Shaytāni 'r-rajīm* and, *Bismillāhi 'r-Raḥmāni 'r-Raḥīm.* We may use it or we can't save ourselves. Therefore, always try to say, *aʿūdhu billāhi min ash-Shaytāni 'r-rajīm* and, *Bismillāhi 'r-Raḥmāni 'r-Raḥīm.* If you are not hearing and obeying, you must look (at what is) going to happen to you before the Last Days, before the Day of Resurrection. *Astaghfirullāh, astaghfirullāh, astaghfirullāh, astaghfirullāh, astaghfirullāh.*

I was in Madinat al-Munawwara and saw a moon eclipse, and I heard from the minarets of the holy city some strange sounds, deeply saying, *astaghfirullāh, astaghfirullāh, astaghfirullāh, astaghfirullāh, astaghfirullāh.* I heard a secret sound I heard when I was in seclusion. I heard on 15 Rajab that eclipse happened; a secret sound through the minarets of the Prophet's ﷺ holy tomb was saying, *astaghfirullāh, astaghfirullāh, astaghfirullāh.*

O People! So many signs are coming and you must say *astaghfirullāh, astaghfirullāh, astaghfirullāh.* Saying the Seal of Prophets ﷺ, "Daily, I am saying 70 times *astaghfirullāh.*" What about for us? Seventy billion times is not enough for us! *Tawbah yā Rabbī, astaghfirullāh. Tawbah yā Rabbī, astaghfirullāh.*

May Allāh ﷻ forgive us.

Fātiḥah.

Ask From Those Who Are Expert

A'ūdhu billāhi min ash-Shaytāni 'r-rajīm. Biṣmillāhi 'r-Raḥmāni 'r-Raḥīm. Dastūr, yā Sayyidī. Madad, yā rijālAllāh!

Stand up for your Lord, for our Creator, Allāh almighty, Most Beneficent and Most Magnificent. *Allāhu Akbar, Allāhu Akbar, Allāhu Akbar, lā ilāha illa-Llāh, Allāhu Akbar, Allāhu Akbar, wa lillāhi 'l-ḥamd*! O our Lord, forgive us! O our Lord, we are asking for Your blessings! O our Lord, don't leave us with our dirty egos. Give Your heavenly support for Your weak servants! We are asking humbly all praising and all glory for Your most honored one in Your Divinely Presence, Sayyidīna Muḥammad ﷺ! We are against Shaytān's people who do not give their high respect to You! You are respecting Sayyidīna Muḥammad ﷺ, but so many no-mind, no-honor people and followers of Shaytān don't like that we are giving our high respect!

We are saying first of all, *a'ūdhu billāhi min ash-Shaytāni 'r-rajīm, Bismillāhi 'r-Raḥmāni 'r-Raḥīm,* and the first lesson is that Man must learn to say this. O our Lord, shelter us from evil and devils, and making people unhappy. People asking to be happy here and Hereafter, but they are not asking how they can reach to that pleasure and enjoyment and Divinely Presence, and they are not asking how heavenly grants will reach to them.

O our Grandshaykh ق, the master of this world, in spite of Shaytāns and their followers, (taught us to say) *a'ūdhu billāhi min ash-Shaytāni 'r-rajīm. Bismillāhi 'r-Raḥmāni 'r-Raḥīm.* That is heavenly sword that we must use! It is not only for show: *Bismillāhi 'r-Raḥmāni 'r-Raḥīm* is a real sword! Heavenly sword is not for show, but you must use it against your enemies.

Inna Shaytāna lakum 'adūwun fatakhidhu 'adūwa.

Verily Satan is an enemy to you, so treat him as an enemy. 35:6

O *'ulama* from Arab brothers, think on it, think on it, what Allāh Almighty saying your language is Arabs and you may understand more and more but you are sleeping not asking what does it mean. O, I am entering Haramayn Sharifayn in Meccatu 'l-Mukarrama and in Madinatu 'l-Munawwara. *Yā Rabbī zidhuma,* give more honor and more lights, more *nūr*!

Those two *masjids* that one of them the first one put on Earth to be prayer place.

Inna awwala baytin wudiʿa lin-nāsi lal-ladhībi-bakkata mubārakan wa hudan lil-ʿAlamīn.

The first House (of worship) appointed for Men was that at Bakkah, full of blessing and guidance for all kinds of beings. 3:96

Listen and look to me and you may understand that I am blaming first those people from Arab Muslims who are claiming they are *ʿulama,* learned ones, that no one else can understand. I am asking, "What you are understanding, *awwalu yawm* (first day)? You are ʿAbdAllāh, *SubḥānAllāh* for ʿAbdAllāh, Allāh Almighty putting a symbol, symbolizing what? What is Allāh Almighty symbolizing with Baytullāh? Baytullāh is something that you must understand, because you have been ordered to go and pray there.

The first man, Adam; do you think Allāh Almighty has only one Adam and only one Baytullāh? What do you think, O our *ʿulama;* what you are understanding? *Inna awwala baytin wudiʿa lin-nāsi lal-ladhībi bakkata mubārakan wa hudan lil-ʿAlamīn.* Where is that praying area honored for being place of worshipping the Lord of Creation? O Salafi *ʿulama*! do you think that Allāh ﷻ has only one *bayt, awwala baytin?* Just it is for honoring that holy place, from pre-Eternal up to Eternal. How many Abraham?

Wa minhum man lam naqsus ʿalayka.

And some whose story We have not related to thee." 40:78

Are you understanding *Qur'ani 'l-Karīm,* O Salafi *ʿulama*! are you understanding what our Lord, Almighty Allāh, is saying about prophets? What is that? The Lord ﷻ is saying, "I sent *anbīyā,* prophets. Some of them I am saying their names clearly and showing some of their lives clearly, but some others I am keeping hidden. I am not saying their names or what their missions were, where they have been sent, or when their prophethood was. I am not speaking about their lives or their nations."

Because that is a sign when Allāh Almighty says, *Wa minhum man lam naqsus ʿalayka.* "I am not giving knowledge about their names, their nations, their worlds, where they have been, what they said or did. That is closed." That means there are countless, because from pre-Eternal up to Eternal, prophets are never stopping; they are continuous!

Awwala Baytin, "First House" is which one? Before *Awwala Baytin,* was there no place for praying? From where was that holy house of our Lord brought and put there? Who knows? Where was it before? Do you think that it is only a simple building or are you trying to understand it? When Allāh Almighty is in existence, He is *Azāliyūn,* without beginning and end. Do you think He was also *Rabbun yʿubad* at that time? Before Sayyidīna Ibrahim ﷺ placed that house on Meccatu 'l-Mukarrama, wasn't there any *bayt* before that for Allāh ﷻ? Was it just put for His servants to pray and *taʿabud,* worship? What was before that, nothing?

O People! O *ʿulama*! If you are going to learn something, Allāh Almighty is saying:

fās'al bīhī khabīrā.

Ask Him, as He is al-Khabir. *25:59*

If you can't reach *haqīqatu 'l-amr,* reality of that one, you must ask someone who knows about that *khabīr. Khabīr* is *mubālagha,* " to exaggerate." That means "no one is knowing." Who is not knowing, must ask such a person. Because someone may know. So many countless wisdoms and knowledges and news has just happened or will happen on the level of Creation.

fās'al bīhī khabīrā. Don't ask who are so proud, saying, "We are doctors." What do you know? Do you think you ask something from such a person who knows? Who knows what you are asking? Whom you ask must be *khabīr,* expert! How many experts, only one?

O Salafi *ʿulama*! You know nothing because you are not asking a *khabīr,* expert, to tell you some secret knowledge. Is there no secret knowledge; all knowledge is open? What do you think about Sayyidīna Musa ﷺ? That addressing was also coming to him, because for everything he was thinking on it. But he was unable to find treasures, or he found treasures but not the key to open them. Therefore, Allāh Almighty said, *fās'al bīhī khabīrā.* You must ask who knows what you don't know. And Sayyidīna Musa ﷺ ran to find that person who has secrets about so many things! Countless knowledge oceans, the key was with him. Who was that? Sayyidīna Khidr ﷺ was *khabīr,* and Sayyidīna Musa ﷺ was not *khabīr*. Therefore, Allāh Almighty is saying, *fās'al bīhī khabīrā.*

Saḥābah ʿalayhimu 'r-ridwān were asking from Sayyidīna Rasūlullāh ﷺ. *Anbīyā* were asking from whom? Who is the teacher of prophets? Sayyidīna

Muḥammad ﷺ is the teacher for everything in existence! He is that *khabīr*, who knows that only Allāh ﷻ knows. He does not know all what Allāh Almighty knows; he only knew some knowledge granted to him for a handful of people, or worlds or hegemony.

Dominion Oceans will open to you endlessly; if you need something through life, you must ask who knows. *fās'al bīhī khabīrā*. They are all *khabīr*, knowing what no one knows.

> *Shahida Allāhu annahu lā ilāha illa huwa wa 'l-malāʿikatu wa ūlū al-ʿilmi qā'imān bil-qisti lā ilāha illa huwa al-ʿazīzu 'l-hakīm.*
>
> *There is no god but He! That is the witness of Allāh, His angels, and those endued with knowledge, standing firm on justice. There is no god but Him, the Exalted in Power, the Wise.* 3:18

O Salafi *ʿulama*! You are not *khabīr*, so why are you so proud, saying, "We are graduated from Meccatu 'l-Mukarrama's university, Jāmiʿatu Islāmiyya fi 'l-Hijāz." Do their teachers know everything? Why aren't they asking for *utlubu 'l-ʿilm?*

Don't say, "We graduated, now there is nothing else to learn." That is your ignorance. You must learn that. A weak one going to teach you, a weak one that his Arabic is nothing, by holy command from Heavens, *fās'al bīhī khabīrā*. You must understand. I am asking, *awwala baytin wudiʿa lin-nāsi lal-ladhī bibakkata mubārakan. Bakkata* or *Makkata*? What is between *Bakkata* and *Makkata? fās'al bīhī khabīrā.*

For understanding we are going to libraries. What does it mean? No, *ʿilm* is a living grant from Allāh Almighty to His servants. The Seal of Prophets ﷺ wasn't reading books and learning; *ʿilm* is a heavenly grant from our Lord to whom He likes.

Once Fakhrūddīn Razī ؓ, a famous commentator, was visiting *awwala baytin wudiʿa lin-nāsi* and people ran to him to take some benefit or to reach some lights from his knowledge. Because knowledge is not a material thing, it is a heavenly grant and a heavenly grant is *nūr*, light. People were running to know and understand something about unknown oceans of knowledge. He was sitting and people were giving him their high respect. Imām Razī ؓ spoke in front of Kaʿbah and they were looking at a *khabīr* who knows so many things that others don't know.

And he was sitting a *kursī*, throne or chair. All people were standing up to honor and for his respect. Only one person was sitting there, covering his head, sitting, never moving. And Fakhrūddīn Razī ♣, Allāh ﷻ bless him, was looking around and everyone was standing up, and only that one in front of Kaʿbah never changed his face or never stood up. He was saying, "Who is that one like me, a person coming here and not giving his respect? At least he should have respect for my knowledge." This was passing through his heart.

After he was left that one. I must leave him, I must address to our listeners. He tried to speak but was not able to say anything. Like me, beginning to cough. I am really coughing but he was saying, people were looking, "O People! I can't address you, something happening here now that I am not able to address you." And he was showing that person who is that one. "Because of that one my heart is just locked and my tongue can't be able to say anything."

He ran to that one and asking, "O our master, did I do something wrong? Please forgive me, I don't know what I am going to say to people, I knew so many things but now my tongue is just locked. I can't speak, please forgive me!" And he was kissing his hands saying. "O this is Baytullāh for the honor for that Baytullāh forgive me," and he was saying "O People! that one who looking from east to west, from north to south through oceans and continents is sitting here. I am asking for forgiveness in front of you." And he is saying, "Go and speak, enough for you what you said now, we are opening."

Khabīr was Sayyidīna Muḥīyiddīn Ibn al-ʿArabī ق; Fakhrūddīn Razī ق knew nothing in front of that one. He was an ocean and Fakhruddin was a drop. A drop how swimming in it? That was ocean, oceans asking *madad*, support, asking some grants through Heavens from that one. "How can I speak to you?" Now he opened I may speak to you.

O Salafi and Wahabi *ʿulama*! They are bringing to me to speak to you *khāsah*, a special addressing to Arab *ʿulama* who think they are something special, and they are nothing until asking from that *khabīr*.

O People! You must try to learn something. This planet is like an atom through bigness, greatness of existence, of divinely dominions. Through Divine Dominions our world, this planet, it is such an atom or less. Ask for more! Ask for more, *fās'al bīhī khabīrā wa qul Rabbī zidnī ʿilma. "And say (O Muḥammad!), O my Lord increase me in knowledge."* (20:114) *Khitāb*, addressing Allāh Almighty to His most beloved one and saying "Ask for more knowledge!" Endless knowledge oceans, wisdom oceans belong to Me. Ask Me, *wa qul Rabbī zidnī ʿilma*!

Yes, why are you not asking? Why are you saying this one who puts a turban on his head doesn't have knowledge? Try to learn and keep your *adab*. don't say, "This one." No, all of us are on the same level, created as the Children of Adam ﷺ. Don't think you are something important or you will never be an important one; you will remain on the level of ignorance. Try to learn that endless oceans of knowledge are put in an atom:

Huwa ʿalā kulli shay'in qadīr.

He has power to do all things. *67:1*

O my Lord! Forgive Your servants and send one who may teach us and help us to understand heavenly secrets, for understanding secrets of creating, the secrets granted from the Lord of Heavens to His creatures and particularly what Mankind is granted of knowledge. He is giving to them; try to make it more as you are not going to forget such knowledge. Real knowledge can't leave you, but artificial knowledge will leave you and you will become a naked tree with nothing on it; no flowers, leaves or fruits.

May Allāh ﷻ forgive us.

Fātiḥah.

Discipline Your Ego by Learning

A'ūdhu billāhi min ash-Shaytāni 'r-rajīm. Bismillāhi 'r-Raḥmāni 'r-Raḥīm. Dastūr, yā Sayyidī. Madad, yā rijālAllāh!

La ilāha illa-Llah, lā ilāha illa-Llāh, lā ilāha illa-Llāh Muḥammad Rasūlullāh, 'alayhi salātullāh 'alayhi salāmullāh. Lā ilāha illa-Llāh, lā ilāha illa-Llāh, lā ilāha illa-Llāh, Muḥammad habībullāh 'alayhi salātullāh, 'alayhi salāmullāh. O our Lord, forgive us, and bless your weak servants and we are saying thousands and thousands of praisings and glory on your most honored servant, Sayyidīna Muḥammad ﷺ! For his honor forgive us, O our Lord!

O People! Stand up and give your highest respect and glorifying and praising for the Lord of Heavens, for the Lord of all Creations from pre-Eternal up to Eternal.

Dastūr yā RijālAllāh, madad. O Awlīyā, O holy ones honored in the heavenly presence of the Seal of Prophets ﷺ! We are asking from our master, *quṭb* of this planet, who is looking towards the heavenly presence, and looking again for their missions and priorities. When that *quṭb* looks for this planet, his looking is for everything on it, never making him to be occupied with anything else, in order to be in the Heavenly Presence of the Lord of Heavens.

Lā yashghilhu shāni shānun an shān. "One affair does not keep Him busy from attending another;" they are created in perfection. Their spirituality or spiritual being can't leave its position in the Heavenly Presence of the Lord of Heavens. And at the same time, they are using another position to arrange everything on this planet. Everything must be under their control! That is their honor. Their hearts are never going to leave the Heavenly Presence of the Lord of Heavens.

Therefore, the Lord of Heavens is saying, *qalbu 'l-mu'min 'arshullāh,* "The Heart of the believer is the Throne of God." Their heavenly being, *qalb,* is not a piece of flesh. This is only to make our bodies to work as is necessary, to control everything. Therefore, when the heart is a little bit upset, the whole body is upset. Therefore, this piece of flesh controls everything for Mankind through their physical being, and it is under his control. Sending. Without someone sending, do you think that our blood can move or can know where it is going or what is its importance?

Some of our blood is running up to our heads and that is different from that coming to our eyes. And that power that our heart is using or sending; everything is in its real position. Everything just planned and can't be in a wrong way; must be 100% in perfection. Who is sitting in your heart and controlling you? One holy one! The Lord of Heavens gives authority to that one who is controlling Mankind on this planet.

And at the same time, there are other holy ones under the *quṭb*'s command, belonging to that one, to look for after every Creation on Earth. There can't be any wrong action, any wrong movement, any wrong being on it; everything must be in its perfect position. When losing that perfection, Man may fall sick, or he loses control on his physical being passes away. That power was taken up from that person.

Therefore, Allāh Almighty is *Subḥān*. Everything is in highest position and highest perfection through every Creation. Everything must be under a power station. Look, one atom. Do you think that atom is moving by itself? And its creation is by itself ? Or a grant to it from outside. Or, they are preparing by themselves to be hydrogen atom, or oxygen atom, or iron atom? They are saying that there are 104 or 105 kinds of atoms. Do you think that they can't be more, or can't be less? Or in opposite. May be, an atom in an opposite direction. Two directions, up or down. By itself? And our scientists or chemists or physicist's are only knowing the Mendeleev system. The Lord of Heavens under a control? Mendeleev was saying that there will be 99 elements. Really 99, but they are trying to make it more. They can't do. No permission for them. Therefore, they are trying to make one more and that is going to be an artificial atom. An artificial atom is an imitated being in existence. You can't do this. Therefore, they are taking the reasons of being an element; sometimes, if that power is taken from it, just disappearing. And Allāh Almighty's power, *qudrah*, His Might, can't be in limits. That is *musakhkhar*, just granted to Man to run in it; as a circle. "You may be in this," enjoy yourself. Allāh may do whole world through one atom's circle and may say to all people: you do as you like here. This bigness that we are seeing can be in limits through an atomic being. He is Allāh!

O our Listeners! Use your minds. Think on it. To think for something through creation, Prophet ﷺ saying, *Tafakkaru sa'atin khayrun min 'ibādati saba'īna sanah*, "To think about deepless limits of Creation, even one hour is good for you than to make 70 years praying." Because you can pray heedlessly for 70 years and never understand anything the Lord of Heavens is saying. *SubḥānAllāh*! Glory for Allāh!

O our Salafi *ʿulama*! What do you think when Allāh Almighty says:

Wa mā khalaqtu 'l-jinna wa 'l-insa illa li yʿabudūn.

I created Jinn and Mankind only to worship Me. 51:56

Giving meanings of *illa li yʿabudūn, li yʿarifūn, nihāyatu ʿindahu li yaʿrafūnī*! I granted them such a power that with it they may reach through knowledge of My Own Being, *mʿarifatullāh: wa mā khalaqtu 'l-jinna wa 'l-ins illa li yʿabudūn*. That is one of the most important Power Oceans for creation, especially for Mankind: *wa mā khalaqtu 'l-jinn wa 'l-ins*. Why jinn is first and Man second? I am asking them to say something to me, but they can't say. Therefore, we are using holy words of Allāh Almighty. If you don't know:

fās'al bīhī khabīrā.

Ask you then about Him from any acquainted (with such things). 25:59

Nothing can be unknown in the level of servanthood. Closed for servants. You only know a servanthood level that is necessary for yourself, *tʿadhīman*; by glorifying the Lord. All knowledge that was granted through holy books to prophets and from prophets to common people, for what? To differentiate, *li yʿarifūn*. That level for all Creation; level "*ʿuqūl*," which means, those who are granted an understanding through their minds and mentalities.

The summary of whole messengerhood or prophethood is on two points: one, the level of servants; they are granted knowledge through heavenly ones; they are prophets, teaching them about their existence, about their creation, about their missions. This teaching is one level and they are learning on it only. They must know this. Up (above this level,) is only for Allāh and that, no one knows about. They are not responsible for that knowledge. We are only learning through prophets. Their prophecy is teaching people about themselves, about their beings, about their missions, about their purpose; for what they have been created. That level and not above it.

Li yʿarifūn means, I only created Jinn and Man for understanding their Creator; there is a Creator who created us and He is always from pre-Eternal up to Eternal an Unknown One. What we know is only *tʿadhīm*, glorifying. We must know that there is a Sulṭān, but *hawiyya*, the identity is impossible for us to know. We only must learn that there is our Lord and we must give our endless glorifying to Him. How can we do that? That is level of teaching: *fās'al bīhī khabīrā.* Common people are on that level. They know nothing, therefore, the Lord of Heavens is sending us special or selected ones. Dressing such a power, that no one can be able to come close for understanding.

What are Salafi *ʿulama* saying? What do you think the holy words that Allāh Almighty is saying, mean.

W 'attaqullāha wa yuʿallimukumullāh.

So fear God, for it is God Who teaches you. *2:282*

What does it mean? You are thinking that knowledge is only through the writing of any book? No, that book is not teaching you, but the teacher; specialized, chosen people, because they are keeping as they can carry, to make their last glorifying to Him. Then they will be granted from heavenly ones such knowledge that common people can't reach. Therefore, '*'ulama,'* are learned people, not learning from books but their teacher. The Lord of Heavens is saying: *w 'attaqullāha wa ʿallimukumullāh.*

Ar-Raḥmān ʿallama 'l-Qur'an.

The Most Merciful, taught the Qur'an. *55:1-2*

Not Jibrīl bringing, but teaching; Who was teacher of Sayyidīna Muḥammad ﷺ? His teacher is his Lord, Almighty Allāh!

O People! try to learn. The worst label for Man is to be ignorant. Written on millions of people, angels just putting a label: "ignorant." And written for those whom asking to learn and they are paying something for learning, when you are going to school, paying fees. What they are paying? They are paying by giving their egos back and taking in front of their egos, *nūr,* through their hearts. And the blood from their hearts is running everywhere with *nūr.* If a person is not hearing in every cell, he can't learn anything from Allāh Almighty's teaching. Every cell and everything in a cell; so many kinds of beings in a cell, they must be ready for understanding then they may understand something. Allāh is teaching those people, not like ourselves, *hasharāt,* the lowest level creatures; He is teaching the best ones. Therefore, the best ones in all Creation are prophets, and the best of all is only Sayyidīna Muḥammad ﷺ! Allāh ﷻ is saying, *ar-Raḥmān ʿallama 'l-Qur'an.*

O our Salafi *ʿulama*! Where are you and where is your Lord? You say you know Qur'an; who is teaching you? You think that Allāh is teaching you? He taught His most beloved one. Even Sayyidīna Jibrīl learned from him because the closest one in the Divine Presence was Sayyidīna Muḥammad ﷺ. Stand up!

O People! this is a deepless ocean. Such things. The Lord of Heavens is asking to change everything on Earth now, because last days are approaching! The Day of Resurrection is coming and just granted, such pure people who are on steps of the Seal of Prophets ﷺ. Learning and teaching. Last chance for Mankind! The Lord of Heavens is asking to clean them. Therefore, two labels: on one label is written: "ignorant," second:

Forgive us! This is an endless ocean, a little bit more and people can't carry. O Man, oceans, oceans, oceans. Through oceans, new appearances; through oceans, new visions; through oceans, new lightening territories. *Allāhu Akbar, Allāhu Akbar*! O People! don't waste your time with this dirty life. Why is it dirty? Because they are killing each other, that is the biggest sin. For a Man to kill another man, biggest sin! Allāh Almighty saying: O bad servant, do you think that I ordered to you to kill someone and they are innocent? My Divine anger on you. I am sending on you if you killed one, to be killed up to end of the world, every moment.

N'audhubillāh, O People! don't kill, don't try to make new weapons for killing thousands and millions people. Allāh Almighty will take His revenge on those people because they are oppressors and disobedient, and the worst servants!

May Allāh ﷻ forgive us.

Fātiḥah.

Those With Knowledge Truly Fear Allah

A'ūdhu billāhi min ash-Shaytāni 'r-rajīm. Biṣmillāhi 'r-Raḥmāni 'r-Raḥīm. Dastūr, yā Sayyidī. Madad, yā rijālAllāh!

Dastūr yā Sayyidī, madad. Yā Allāh. Lā ilāha illa-Llāh, lā ilāha illa-Llah, lā ilāha illa-Llāh Muḥammadun Rasūlullāh, 'alayhi salātullāh, 'alayhi salāmullāh. Lā ilāha illa-Llāh, lā ilāha illa-Llāh, lā ilāha illa-Llāh Muḥammadun Habībullāh, 'alayhi salātullāh, 'alayhi salāmullāh! All praising and whole glorifying is only for You, O our Lord! You are our Creator. Forgive us and send us from heavenly winds on our bodies and on our spiritual being to be every time fresh! That is for You, *yā Rabbi 'l-'izzati wa 'l-'adhāmati wa 'l-Jabarūt*! And endless salute and *salāms* on Your most honored one, for whom You created all Creation for his honor, Sayyidīna Muḥammad ﷺ. Grant to him, O our Lord! Forgive us O our Lord, and support us for his honor.

As-salāmu 'alaykum our visitors, our listeners! Welcome to you. You are not coming to me. You are asking to reach heavenly stations, so that every time you are getting up and getting lighter, and the heaviness of your physical being leaving yourselves. Therefore, praying and worshipping is taking away from people the heavy burdens that just put on their shoulders.

O our Salafi *'ulama*, what do you think Allāh Almighty is saying? *Asta'idh billāh. Inna 'aradna 'l-amānata 'alā 's-samāwati wa 'l-'ardi wa 'l-jibāli.* It is Arabic or Turkish? (It is) Arabic, *lisānu 'l-Qur'ani 'l-Karīm* and you are more worthy for understanding Arabic. Allāh Almighty is saying:

> *Inna 'aradna 'l-amānata 'alā 's-samāwati wa 'l-ardi wa 'l-jibāli fa'abayna an yahmilnaha wa ashfaqna minha wa hamalaha 'l-insān innahu kāna dhalūman jahūlah.*
>
> *We did indeed offer the Trust to the Heavens and the Earth and the mountains, but they refused to take it, being afraid thereof; but Man undertook it. Indeed, he was unjust and foolish!* 33:72

Allāh Almighty is saying to the Heavens, "Have full spirituality and nothing of material heaviness," and He is saying to the whole Earth, "This is My *amānaha*, grant." "Grant" is not a full description in other languages for what Allāh Almighty is saying, *amānah*. "I am just granting from My holy

Heavens full with holiness." Heavens have lights reflecting on them from the Divine Presence.

Madad yā Sulṭān al-Awlīyā, madad! If you are not reaching to weak servants no one can speak on such fine subjects! If the Lord of Heavens was not giving an ability for carrying His Oath, it would be heavy and impossible. O our Grandshaykh, our Master! Make it easy for your servant and for all Creation in this world for understanding something. You are responsible on that point and we are coming, *muwājahah,* to your holy beings appearance, because you are such a powerful one.

It is impossible for common people to look at them with these eyes. Our physical eyes can't be able to approach and look at them. Only whom their inner eyes are open may look. Looking is something, understanding is something else, and to be with that understanding is something else from being in that holy position that just dressed on them.

O Man, O Human Beings! Don't think that you are a simple creation or simple being. What was Sayyidīna ʿAli ق saying? *Tadhunnu annaka jirmun saghīr wa fīka natwi al-ʿalim al-Akbar,* "Do you think you are a speck when the whole universe is contained in you?" Yes, Sayyidīna ʿAli ق was saying, you think you are a so small creation through one-and-a-half and two meters. That is *wasat,* the medium measure of our physical being. If we are coming down from one-and-a-half meters, going to be ugly; also, if passing over two meters, a giant, huge person, going to be ugly. So Allāh Almighty created Man in such a perfect form: too small one or too long one would be ugly, making in such a way that there is perfection in it. *SubhānAllāh*! There is one word to describe it: *amlāq,* giant. Therefore, Allāh Almighty is saying, *astaʿidh billāh*:

Laqad khalaqnal insāna fī ahsani taqwīm.

We have indeed created Man in the best of molds. *95:5*

You can't imagine for a Man or woman another form to look beautiful or handsome. What do you think if you are granted four legs? People now running after *dunyā* so much and they are saying two legs are not enough! What do you think if you have four legs? You will be like a giraffe, so long. What about if your tallness going to be like giraffe? No good, three meters or four meters? You may collect everything without using stairs or ladders. What do you think about it? You will answer, "No, I don't like it."

What about if you will be weight lifter? Now people make *musābaqah,* competitions of who can carry the heaviest weight. I am saying if you are asking for a competition, make that competition with a donkey; it is always carrying what you are carrying two-times more. You must not put this gold medal for you, you must put it on the neck of the donkey. The donkey is going to be very happy, saying, "I am champion!"

Is anyone much more powerful than a donkey? Who is carrying heavy burden to make a proof that you are more powerful than a donkey? No, never! A donkey is always more powerful than you. You may only carry and your legs are trembling; you can't move even one step. But a donkey, if putting two times more than you, is carrying on its back and it may go.

O People! No one can think of a form, *sūrah,* more perfect. Angels have wings, but what do you think their out-looking or their creation is more important than our creation? No, nothing in existence can reach the perfection that Allāh Almighty granted to Mankind. Where is your thanks, O Mankind? You are not happy that Allāh Almighty created you a man and not a donkey? And always you are complaining? Complaining for what? Because Allāh Almighty not creating you to be a donkey? Why you are complaining? You must say, "Thanks my Lord, that You chose me to be from the Children of Adam, and Adam is created in such perfection that no other Creation may reach his perfection." You are not ashamed, O Mankind, to complain? For what? That you are not created as a donkey, a dog or fox?!

Therefore, we are saying that is heavenly knowledge from prophets to their real followers. Such knowledge granted to make people to wake up; *taqdīr,* to appreciate what Allāh granted to them. Allāh is saying, "I am asking to load My Divine oath on worlds, on Heavens," and they say, "O our Lord, forgive us, *fa'abayna an yahmilnaha,* If You are leaving it for our will, we are asking for forgiveness. *Wa hamalaha 'l-insān.*"

O Salafi *'ulama*! What was it that Allāh Almighty asked to put; what was that *amānah*? You can tell me? Don't speak always on *shirk* and *kufr*! Teach people from real knowledge, then they should know what is *harām* and what is *halāl.* All prophets came to teach people what is forbidden and what is permitted. Try to learn that, then tell me, "We are Salafi *'ulama.*" Tell me what was that *amānah* that all Heavens and Earth were trembling and also gigantic mountains like Himalayan Mountains, were going to be a *sahal,* flat, saying, "O our Lord, we can't carry it!" What was that? You know or you don't know?! If you don't know, Allāh is saying, *fās'al bīhī khabīrā,* "Ask those who know."

Once again we are saying look throughout the east and west for someone to tell you or to teach you, but don't think that they are granting such precious jewels to anyone. What do you think? You are very rich people; Saudi people have too many jewels: rubies, emeralds, diamonds, pearls, sapphires and so many others. What do you think? Would you like to put that necklace on the neck of a donkey? Say to me, yes? Say to me and I am giving an answer to you. You think you know everything but you know nothing! Because they are trying to put that precious necklace on such people who are *mustawa*, at the level of donkeys!!

What do you think if you are putting a necklace of precious stones on the neck of a donkey; is it getting a value? No. Therefore, do you think that such precious knowledge is granted for everyone? No, that is a grant from the Lord of Heavens. You are not graduating even one student if he did not reach perfection on his branch. And do you think the Lord of Heavens is giving to you the Holy Qur'an, full with jewels a hundred times the value of this universe? What you are saying?

Wa hamalahal insān. Inna aradna 'l-amānata ala 's-samāwāti wa 'l-ardi wa 'l-jibāli fa'abayna an yahmilnaha. O our Lord, if You are giving that trust in your necks, some thief, some robber or crook may take from us. This must be granted to someone that he can be able to keep those jewels. You are not on that level. Therefore, Allāh Almighty, not giving to you. Don't say, "We are Salafi *ʿulama*." Where is *ʿulama*? Allāh saying: *innamā yakhshaL'laaha min ʿibādihi 'l -ʿulama. Those who have knowledge truly fear Allāh.* (35:28)

You are looking yourself on that level that Allāh Almighty asking? Do you think that you have such a *khushū'*? Do you think that when you say, *Allāhu Akbar*, your whole organs trembling? You are not on that level; therefore, not granted yet. Don't say, "We are Salafi *ʿulama*." No!

You may ask, "How we can reach that level, that Allāh Almighty praised them?" Not everyone granted that trembling from *khashyatillāh*, heavenly fear mixed up with *taʿdhīm wa takrīm*, glorifying and praising. Don't think that when you are wearing *abaya* (cloak) and putting around your clothes golden or silver ornaments that you are something!

It is a short story I like to say to those people who are looking always to their clothes or their crowns and getting proud. At the time of Sulṭān Timur, who was coming from Middle Asia to edges of European borders, he met there Mūllah Nasrūddīn. "Mūllah" really means *mawla*. It is as a *mūllah*, ʿAtīqu 'r-Rahman, from whom Allāh Almighty ordered no account or questioning on the Day of Resurrection. Allāh Almighty gives everyone a specialty, and the specialty of Mūllah Nasrūddīn was to make people laugh and think.

One day Mūllah Nasrūddīn was in a Turkish bath with Sulṭān Timur Khan, who said, "O Mūllah Nasrūddīn! If I was a slave-servant, what do you think my price would be if taking me to the market of maidens?"

Mūllah Nasrūddīn answered, "O Your Majesty, you will have ten *dirhams.*"

"What you are saying, O Mūllah Nasrūddīn? Only ten *dirhams* for me? This sarong alone cost ten *dirhams*. What about for me?"

Mūllah Nasrūddīn said, "No value for you. No one gives for you any *dirham.* I was saying only for that sarong, not for you. Who is going to buy you and your foot is crooked? (Timur Khan was lame). Who will take you?"

And the sulṭān was laughing, so happy. But really Mūllah Nasrūddīn was giving a lesson to Man. Everyone thinks when they are dressing in such ornaments they will be so valuable. No. If looking, no one will pay even one *riyal*.

O People! Listen and try to learn something that helps you here and Hereafter, making your ego down and heavenly ornaments coming on you. O People! Don't lose praise at their times. First is Allāh Almighty's command; after it, you may look for your provisions. Don't live only for your provision but try to live as a servant of the Lord of Heavens! May Allāh ﷻ forgive us.

May Allāh ﷻ forgive us.

Fātiḥah.

Every Living Thing Praises Allah

A'ūdhu billāhi min ash-Shaytāni 'r-rajīm. Bismillāhi 'r-Raḥmāni 'r-Raḥīm. Dastūr, yā Sayyidī. Madad, yā rijālAllāh!

Lā ilāha illa-Llāh, lā ilāha illa-Llāh, lā ilāha illa-Llāh Muḥammadun Rasūlullāh. O our Lord, You are our Creator! Only You are saying Your holy order, "Be" and anything is coming into existence. You are asking anything You like to disappear from existence. If You say, "Go back, don't be in existence!" that is finished! All Creation, less than a third or down, down, down in a part the smallest time may disappear, everything.

O People! Give your most high glorifying and most high praises to our Lord, that His order is only between, "Be" and "Don't be." O our Lord, forgive us! We are asking Your most high glorifying in Creation from pre-Eternal up to Eternal, Your most beloved servant, the king of Your creatures from pre-Eternal up to Eternal is Sayyidīna Muḥammad ﷺ!

O People! We know nothing. We know nothing until the Lord of Heavens is asking for His creatures to know something. Everything in existence must know their Creator. Can't be atoms and less atoms; all of them must know Who created them and they must give their highest glorifying to their Creator.

O our Salafi *'ulama*! What are you saying to this? What is your opinion? No opinion on dominions! You are asking a proof for that and *a'ūdhu billāhi min ash-Shaytāni 'r-rajīm*. I am running from Shaytān's tricks and to fall in his traps. Therefore, I am asking for a support that is supporting my smallest being against Shaytān and *shaytānic* works. I am saying also *Bismillāhi 'r-Raḥmāni 'r-Raḥīm*. The sword of Heavens was granted to Man, and I am asking from my master, master of this planet, *quṭb*, the pole of this planet, and I am asking for a support from his holy power. If he is not giving permission, I can't speak to you and I can't address anyone. I am going to be the weakest one. I must ask, "O my master! Let us know something from what you are granting to our small group, and addressing from east to west and north to south, to declare a heavenly declaration for creatures."

In this discussion, we are beginning by asking Wahabi or Salafi *'ulama, ma qawlukum*, "What is your opinion?" No opinion. There is reality. Don't say according to my opinion, no. No opinion to you. We are not accepting (anyone who says) "my opinion," no. Your answer must come from heavenly beings, that they are speaking real truth to make our hearts find a full satisfaction. If they are not giving that satisfaction, nothing may give you a satisfaction in your heart. Therefore, don't say to me, "According to my knowledge," or, "According to my opinion," no.

It is such a wire without running in it power of electricity. If not running, what is that wire? Nothing? Yes. There is when you are clicking this lamp and you are cutting the power that is running through wires to that lamp. Lamp by itself can't give a light; no, it is impossible. But it must be granted to give a light to ourselves. Light is also coming from that lamp. From where is it coming? To where is it going? How is it running through wires? Does anyone know? Scientists, do you know? You may say only positive pole and negative pole. That is their last horizon for understanding the power of electricity. They are asking, and we are looking and saying, that power is just appearing through poles: one is negative and one is positive.

O scientists! What is negative and what is positive? To be a sign of positivity, and secondly, they are putting another line and you are saying that is negative pole and that is positive. What is positive and negative beings? From the same spring, source. Different sources, what are those sources? How is that going to be positive and second negative? Who is putting positive of being, that one negative being and that one positive? No one knows? They are saying for understanding that Man just prepared and Man was just created in such a way to understand the reality of being positive or negative.

Finally, we may come to a level that we may even look and we may say that is a positive one, and looking at the other one saying that is a negative one. What does it mean? Positive one, every movement that one is bringing in existence, it is a useful being for the Creation. What about for the negative pole? The negative pole, also it has such a strange being. That is what happening from positive pole, that just going to be used, taken by negative pole and sending away that energy.

As a person is eating, eating what it is giving benefit for person, the body is keeping in it, and what it is not suitable to be protected inside and taken away. That is positive and that is negative, and so on. This means they are under such a way. There is positive understanding and negative one. Positive understanding is granted to your spiritual being and negative side of Man that just taken from it. What it is that is going to be taken from that one, and is going to be empty and thrown out. Now we were saying Allāh Almighty is creating and everything must know their Creator. If their understanding is positive, that is going to be forever. Real reality is granted to that one, and that means truth that belongs to Heavens. There can't be in it any other element for changing it. It is pure power that is making people to understand from reality. Don't think that everything is not going to know Who created them and granted them to be in existence. Everything, even smallest part of matter, must know this and must say *SubḥānAllāh,* "Glory to our Creator," glory to our Creator, glory to our Creator.

O Mankind! What about you? Are you saying, "Glory to our Creator" even once daily? Endless Glory Oceans to our Creator! You are drunk, drinking whiskey, beer, vodka, and champagne, which is making people become so ugly, no-mind ones! Leave that, and come to learn to know about your Creator! Even ants know their Creator; even atoms are recognizing and knowing their Creator, and they are glorifying their Creator saying, *SubḥānAllāh, SubḥānAllāh, SubḥānAllāh,* "Glory to my Creator! Glory to my Creator! Glory to my Creator!"

O People! Today, one day more went away from our lives. We don't know which day is going to be our last day. Sometimes use your mentality. Sometimes use the grant of Heavens that you have been granted from the Lord of Heavens to know Him. Are you using it or not? People are drunk now. That atom is knowing its Creator and what is the proof that they know their Creator?

O Wahabi *ʿulama*! Why are you not saying to people that everything is making *dhikr,* while you are against *dhikr*? Always saying, *bidaʿ, bidaʿ, kufr*. Say to ants also, because they are doing *dhikr*. Are you not reciting the Holy Qur'an? What is it saying?

> *wa in min shay'in illa yusabbihu biḥamdihi, wa lākin lā tafqahūna tasbīhahūm.*
>
> *And there is not a single thing but extols His limitless glory and praise, but you (O Man) fail to grasp the manner of their glorifying Him!* 17:44

min shay'in illa yusabbihu biḥamdihi, "There is not a single thing but extols His limitless glory and praise." Is that *dhikr* or not? Go to ants and other creatures and say, "Don't do that, it is *bidaʿ*." Why are you not saying this? You are coming to me saying, "O Shaykh, you are collecting people and making them to say, *Allāh Allāh, Allāh Allāh, Allāh Allāh, Allāh Allāh, Allāh Allāh, Allāh Allāh, Allāh Allāh.* But you are rushing on people, saying, "If you are making *dhikr*, you are making *shirk*." From where are you bringing this? And you say, "We are *ʿulama*."

If I am collecting people, and making them say all together, *SubḥānAllāh, Sulṭān Allāh, SubḥānAllāh, Sulṭān Allāh, SubḥānAllāh, Sulṭān Allāh*," they are saying, "That is *bidaʿ*." *Dhikr* is *bidaʿ*? From where are you bringing this, so foolishly?! How? From where? What is your proof? Say! You can't say, because you are not using either your mentality or mind, and are never using your heart's power. You will be occupied only with your mind's production. If there is mind's production, much more important is the production of our hearts. Give your hearing for your heart, and try to hear what your heart is saying also! It is saying, *Al-Lah, Al-Lah, Al-Lah, Al-Lah, Al-Lah, Al-Lah, Al-Lah*!

You can't say to me, "No," because Allāh Almighty is saying *wa in min shay'in illa yusabbihu bi-ḥamdihi*. Our heart must say *Allāh, Allāh, SubḥānAllāh. Allāh, Allāh, SubḥānAllāh. Allāh, Allāh, SubḥānAllāh:* the whole world may fall on it. Yes, what we shall do? *Allāhu Akbar*! *Allāhu Akbar*!

You may say over the level of *ʿulama*, look and listen. Don't say, "We know everything." No, you know nothing as I know nothing, but I am giving my heart to hear and something is coming to my ear through my heart, and we are saying something or else I am not knowing also. But such a meaning, it is a grant from the Heavens that believers can understand more and more, because *ʿilm* is a heavenly light granted through heavenly beings to some selected ones of Mankind that are prepared to take that power, heavenly power for hearing and to give. As this, such as scientific instruments, they are hearing and giving. If I am saying a person may listen from heaven, Wahabi *ʿulama* may say it can't be. This manifesting is so easy, so easy, it is nothing. But people are saying, "Ohhh! Technology has just reached the top level."

O *ʿulama*! Why are you not seeing that endless powers have been granted to you from Heavens? Why are you not saying this? If anyone is saying that, you say, "That is *shirk*!" What *shirk*? Take away *kufr* from your books, according to your knowledge. It is not *kufr*! Imām Shahrani said *quṭbs* are not accepting such a thing. But in spite of Wahabis, there is a *quṭb* and people who have been granted heavenly powers. They say if you call a person *"kāfir,"* we must look from which doors coming in, until he is coming from that door out, then we can say he is *kāfir*. Which door are you going and becoming Muslim? The doors of *shahādah*, to say *Ash-hadu an lā ilāha illa-Llah, wa ash-hadu anna Muḥammadan ʿabduhu wa Rasūluh*. According to *Shariʿatullāh* that is a *mu'min*. When does he become *kāfir*? If he is coming out and saying, "I am not believing what I was saying before," then you may say that is a *kāfir*.

Even Holy Qur'an is saying about one Companion of Rasūlullāh ﷺ, that he once killed a person who said, *As-salāmu alaykum*. Rasūlullāh ﷺ was blaming him when he said this word because he feared that the other may kill him. Rasūlullāh ﷺ asked, "Did you open his heart and see that he is not a Muslim?" Even if a person is only saying, *As-salāmu alaykum*, you must say they are Muslim, or *mu'min*. But for everything, Salafi *ʿulama* accuse Muslims of, *"Bidaʿ, kufr, shirk, harām."*

You must know a new period is coming, perhaps the last period of this world. Try to learn *Shariʿat Muḥammadiyyah*. Beware of Shaytān carrying you to the Fire. Follow Salāfu 's-Sālihīn, the ways of *Saḥābah* ﷺ that they are taking from prophets.

O People! Hear and obey. Always blame your ego. Don't try to blame people, (as Salafis) saying, "That is (the way of) *ahlu 'l-bidaʿ*, that is *ahlu 'l-kufr, ahlu 'sh-shirk, ahlu 'l-harām."* Leave that for you (Salafis)! You take care for yourself, because you have not yet been granted a heavenly certificate that you are a real *mu'min* or Muslim on your way to Paradise. Don't do this, and leave people to their Lord! *Allāhu khayrun hāfidhan wa arhamu-rāhimīn wa ahkama'l-hākimīn*. Don't give *hukum*, O Salafi *ʿulama*. Allāh Almighty is warning you and saying, *alaysa 'Llahu bī ahkami 'l-hākimīn*. What we have said, *bela wa akhsah*. Don't be *hakim*, judge on people's actions. Leave them and look after yourself. How it will be the Day of Resurrection?

O People! May Allāh forgive us! Don't say, "Shaykh is singing, *dome, dome*. That is *bidaʿ*." Don't be a judge for anyone! Allāh knows. Because Allāh's Prophet ﷺ was saying, *innama ʿamala bī niyyah*, "Actions are according to their intentions." I am not making *dome, dome* for my ego, no, but to make people happy! Coming a happiness and refreshment to people, to our listeners. *Ka annahu min aswatil samawāt, "It is like a sound from Heaven."*

May Allāh Almighty forgive us, forgive our Salafi *ʿulama*, and forgive everyone as He likes. Thank you for your listening.

O my Listeners! Forgive me also. You say, "At least Shaykh is becoming *kharfān*, too old one. He doesn't know what he is saying. He is not understanding. Therefore, it doesn't matter. We forgive him. It doesn't matter." Ḥadīth Qudsī says, "When My servant reaches 90 years, I forgive him and make him *ʿatīq,* saved. I saved him and he is going to be *ʿuttaqau ʿr-Raḥmān.*" We are on that level. Don't blame me, O young *ʿulama*. No, forgive me, and Allāh ﷻ will forgive you!

May Allāh ﷻ forgive us.

Fātiḥah.

To Listen and Obey Gives Honor

A'ūdhu billāhi min ash-Shaytāni 'r-rajīm. Biṣmillāhi 'r-Raḥmāni 'r-Raḥīm. Dastūr, yā Sayyidī. Madad, yā rijālAllāh!

Dastūr yā Sayyidī, yā Sulṭān al-Awlīyā! Allāhu Akbar, Allāhu Akbar, lā ilāha illa-Llāh, Allāhu Akbar, Allāhu Akbar, wa lillāhi 'l-ḥamd! O our Lord, forgive us! All praising and all glory for You from pre-Eternal up to Eternal, for the honor of Your most honored one in Your Divine Presence, Sayyidīna Muḥammad ﷺ. Give Your most high salutes and glorifying to him as You like. We are under Your holy orders, trying to keep Your holy orders, O our Lord, but we are weak ones. Forgive us for the honor of Sayyidīna Muḥammad ﷺ.

O People! *As-salāmu 'alaykum.* O our listeners, listen to someone authorized to address people and from whom people may understand in their conscience. Hear and listen and obey; that is all prophets' first addressing to people. Come and hear, come and listen, come and obey Him, Who created you. Give your most high glorifying to Him. Don't think that a weak servant may address ten people, ten thousand people, ten million people. May address, even one ant, to ten billion people.

O Salafi *'ulama! As-salāmu 'alā man ittaba'a al-huda.* "Peace to all who follow guidance." (20:47) I was thinking to say, "*As-salāmu 'alaykum,*" but there came a sign to say, *As-salāmu 'alā man ittaba'a al-huda.*

When Allāh Almighty sent Adam and Eve out from Paradise and said to them, "Go live on that planet, *dunyā,* where half is going to be dark, half is going to be lightened," they cried. "You are crying because you lost high-level life filled with pleasures in Paradise. You oppressed yourself, because I was warning you. I made everything in Paradise for you to be *halāl*, the best, permitted. Only one thing, I am not happy for you to eat from that one."

If anyone asks, 'Why?' they will be on the level of Iblīs, Shaytān! Don't ask why!! You can't ask why! No! He is only, *fa'ālu limā yurīd,* "The (sure) Accomplisher of what He plans." (11:107) Who knows what to do, *fa'ālu limā yurīd*. No one can say 'why,' because first that one was saying, "Why I am going to make *sajdah*? I am not making. Who are you?" Iblīs was drunk.

O People! Say, *a'ūdhu billāhi min ash-Shaytāni 'r-rajīm.* You must ask your Lord to shelter you from Shaytān's trips and traps. Don't trust yourself; you can't trust your ego. Allāh Almighty was not trusting Shaytān. Shaytān was praying and trying to do his best for his Lord, and he was thinking something; his main aim was to be Number One in the whole universe. That was a secret aim hiding in his being, because his heart was not like our heart; his creation is different. Man's creation is top level; therefore, Shaytān's heart can't be the same as hearts of the Lord of Heavens' deputies. He wasn't suitable to be successor or deputy as his creation was something else.

Our creation is a special manifestation granted to Man. The Lord was saying, "I am making Adam's physical being with My Hands." What does it mean? What we can understand? Don't think that His Hands are like our hands; it is only a name! He created Man like no other Creation by His Hands! He used His Divine Hands to give form to that new Creation. All creatures on Earth and Heavens are not granted to be deputies, only Man. *ṢubḥānAllāhī 'l-Aliyyi 'l-'Adhīm.* Endless glory is for our Lord. Everything that our Lord makes clear in the Holy Qur'an is according to our understanding level, or no one can understand.

Almighty Allāh was giving special care for Adam's creation when He granted Mankind to be His deputy. Angels did not receive such a special honor, but Allāh Almighty said, "I am making his physical being." Therefore, Man's creation is on the level of *ahsanu khaliqīn,* and best Creator for new creation going to be in the Hands of *ahsanu khaliqīn.* And what He created is *ahsanu taqwīm,* the best *sūrah,* form, out-looking (appearance) and also, only the Lord of Heavens, the Creator of Man, knows his inner creation. Shaytān asked to be on that level, to be deputy in Heavens for Allāh Almighty but his manifestation was not suitable. Therefore, when Allāh Almighty creating Man, just created him in a very special form; a very special being was granted to Mankind.

Iblīs' creation was not *ahsanu taqwīm,* the best form and inner being. He did not know the secret of Adam and asked something that was not for him to ask, *hadha tajawazul haqq* and he was going beyond his limit. That is bad manners from that one. But holy command, He was saying, *usūlu Adam li Adam* (the assets of Adam, to Adam). It was not clear for him. His level of Creation was not suitable and he wasn't created to be deputy for the Lord of Heavens but he was asking. And because he wasn't granted the understanding that the creation of Adam was granted, he asked.

The Lord of Heaven is saying, "Demon, go away."

"How you are saying? Why?"

"Who gives you that authority to ask Me why I am ordering? I am not That One that can be asked by anyone! I am *faʿālu limā yurīd*, That One doing everything as I will. No one can say in My Divine Presence, 'why.' Go away, demon!"

Therefore, all prophets calling Mankind, saying, "Come and hear, come and listen, come and obey!" The Seal of Prophets ﷺ was ordered to collect people on the hill of Safa (in Meccatu 'l-Mukarrama). Allāh Almighty ordered him, "Call people to you." For what? To hear. First command from Heavens to the Last Prophet ﷺ, "Come to the hill of Safa." *Safa* (purity) is a very good word in Arabic. To reach the top of happiness, calling people and people went there, and he ﷺ said, "O People! Hear what I am saying to you. *Lā ilāha illa-Llāh, Muḥammadun Rasūlullāh ʿalayhi 's-salātullāh.*" He ﷺ was calling people, "Hear this from me and repeat it and keep it in your minds. Then when you are hearing, we are sending to who is gathered on this hill some orders. Allāh ﷻ is ordering you to hear and then to listen, *Lā ilāha illa-Llāh, Sayyidīna Muḥammadun Rasūlullāh.*"

Hear, then listen, and the third stage was to obey. That is honor of Mankind: to hear and listen and obey. These three making Paradise to open for those who are hearing and listening and obeying. No way for anyone else to enter Paradise. Who is asking to enter Paradise must hear heavenly words and then must ask, "What does it mean?" Listen. What does it mean, what you are hearing? Then third, the Lord of Heavens is asking, "Obey Me." Be obedient ones to your Creator, to the Lord of Heavens and of everything in existence. But people are running away. Who runs is running away from Paradise and their troubles and miseries and sufferings are beginning in this life. Who are not hearing and listening and obeying, troubles, sufferings, and miseries begin here and run on their head!

O People! Which of you are happy now, or in pleasure, or in enjoyment, or in happiness, or in satisfaction and peace? No one! Not only common people but rich people, powerful people, *sulṭāns*, kings and emperors, are all in trouble, miseries and suffering. No peace now for 21st century people, who lost their happy lives, joyful times and peace. Now people are asking for a peaceful life on this planet. How can it be? If you are not following holy orders, holy commands of Heavens, how can you hope for a peaceful life?

O our Salafi *ʿulama*! What is Allāh Almighty saying? Why you are not saying to everyone, to kings and presidents and prime ministers and commanders? What does it say?

wa man 'arada an dhikrī fa'inna lahu ma`ishatan dankān wa nahshuruhu yawma al-qiyāmati 'ama.

But whosoever turns away from My Reminder, verily, for him is a life of hardship, and We shall raise him up blind on the Day of Resurrection."

20:124

Why you are not saying? You say *dhikr* is *bida*ʿ, and Allāh ﷻ is saying, *wa man 'arada an dhikrī*. What is *dhikr*? *Nabī ʿalayhi 's-salātu was-salām* is Arab. What does he say? *Afdalu dhikrī lā ilāha illa-Llāh, lā ilāha illa-Llāh, lā ilāha illa-Llāh Sayyidīna Muḥammadun Rasūlullāh*!

I don't like for anyone to deny or else throwing something on their heads in this holy month. The first month is Muharram, then Safar is the second month, then *Mawlid an-Nabawi sharīf.* Be careful Salafi *ʿulama* who are following their wrong way, *wa man 'arada an dhikrī*. You are saying it is *bida*ʿ. Don't you know *dhikr* with tongue, *dhikr* with heart? How are you denying that? How? Who is ordering you to say this? And Prophet ﷺ is saying, *ʿalaykum bī 's-sawādu 'l- aʿadham. Ḥadīth* or not? You know everything but you are not saying truth. What do you think?

As-sawādu 'l-aʿadham from the time of this *ummah,* where they are? The great masses of this *ummah;* where they are, you must follow. *As-sawādu 'l-aʿadham* from *ummata Muḥammad* ﷺ. They are denying *dhikr*. How can you deny when Allāh Almighty is saying, *wa man 'arada an dhikrī fa'inna lahu ma`ishatan dankā.* What is *dhikr*? Prophet ﷺ is making clear, "The best *dhikr is Lā ilāha illa-Llah.*" When you are sleeping, your eyes saying, or your nose saying this, or your ears saying this, or by your tongue? I am asking? I am coming to destroy every *bātil,* falsehood, on Earth *bī idhni-Llah,* by Allāh's will!

You are fearing from pig flu, that imagination is a virus, never seen under a microscope. I am not fearing because I am a simple person. Doesn't matter, simple person may sometimes shake east to west and west to east. How it can be? Yes, can be! Because Allāh Almighty giving *taffawuq,* to be high. Sometimes taking from them and giving to western people a highness, but no taste for their highness.

O People! Remember what is being said in such a humble and simple association. I am not claiming anything or I am not asking anything, because my two legs are now in the graveyard. But you are hoping something from *dunyā*. If you are asking something from *dunyā*, you are on the wrong way.

Therefore, Salafi *'ulama*, look what Allāh Almighty is saying, *wa man 'arada an dhikrī fa'inna lahu ma`ishatan dankā*. What do you think of the lifestyle of Muslims now? They are under hegemony of western people or they are over western people? We know that Islamic world is under hegemony of western people, non-Muslims. It is a blame on you to follow them. Now Islamic world is in their worst position, everywhere troubles, miseries, sufferings and killing. And Western people are saying to you, "O Muslims, how you are getting to be in such a bad position?" The answer is from Holy Qur'an, in Sūratu 'l-TaHa (Chapter 20). Who is leaving *dhikr* is given a very heavy life in which they will never be happy!

Look at Palestine, Iraq, Turkey, Egypt, Yemen, Libya, Pakistan and Muslims living in the east and west; some of them are eating others, and running in the streets. In *ḥadīth sharīf,* and all *ḥadīth* are holy, that is our belief, *safwat al-ayyām an-nāsyarkudūna fi 't-turuqāti ka 'l-bahāim wa 'l-wuhūsh bidūn lijām*, "Days will come when people will run in the streets like unbridled beasts."

What is shouting and demonstration in Islam? In what book you are finding 'demonstration' in Islam? Why you are not saying it is *harām*? And they are asking to put their names on top point. That is never going to be for you! Say to people demonstration is forbidden in Islam! I am saying to Iraqi, Palestinian, Egyptian, Turkish, Iranian, Afghani, Pakistani people, demonstration is *harām, harām, harām*! *Al-harāmu bayyinu wa 'l-halālu bayyin.* "*Harām* is clear and *halāl* is clear." If understanding, understand. If not understanding, you will be in the Divine Presence and Allāh Almighty will make His Judgment. We are only giving our announcement to people.

I am a very simple one, not claiming that I am something, no. People are bringing machines and asking me to speak. Heavenly power makes me to speak. I am only a warner. *Innama anā nadhīru 'm-mubīn.* He knows, but you are Arabs, you must look. You must understand, *wa man 'arada an dhikrī fa'inna lahu ma`ishatan dankā*. I am only reminding you that people are losing that, and running in the streets, shouting. For what? Why you are not going to mosques and saying, "O our Lord, save us!" Why you are running like animals in the streets? For what?! I am warning and urging them, "O People! This is *harām*. Go to the mosque and pray to the Lord of Heavens to send you a *sahib*, who may keep the reins of everyone, to bring Islam up and keep *kufr* down."

Wa min Allāhi 't-tawfiq.

I am making music for Salafi and Wahabi *'ulama*! I am happy that I am trying to say what is true, but you are not saying; therefore, you can't sing! (laughter) I am singing, because they are unhappy from it; therefore, I am singing for them again so they may be happy!

May Allāh ﷻ forgive us.

Fātiḥah.

Who Forgets Allah Is Also Forgotten

A'ūdhu billāhi min ash-Shaytāni 'r-rajīm. Biṣmillāhi 'r-Raḥmāni 'r-Raḥīm. Dastūr, yā Sayyidī. Madad, yā rijālAllāh!

Yā Rabbī, anta Rabbī, anta Hasbī! Dastūr yā Sayyidī. For the honor of this holy night, say, Lā ilāha illa-Llāh, lā ilāha illa-Llāh, lā ilāha illa-Llāh, Muḥammad Rasūlullāh 'alayhi salātullāh 'alayhi salāmullāh, 'alayhi ikrāmullāh. As-salāmu 'alayka yā Sayyidīna, yā quṭb, pole of this planet, *as-salāmu 'alayka wa raḥmatūllahi wa barakātuh.*

May Allāh forgive us and bless you for the honor of this holy night. It is a very holy night, the beginning of the New Year 1431. We are asking for this year to be a holy year for the benefit of all Creation. We are saying according holy command of the Lord of Heavens, *a'ūdhu billāhi min ash-Shaytāni 'r-rajīm.* That is our protection from Shaytān, his tricks and traps, so that we do not fall in sewage channels of this dirty life.

O People! *As-salāmu 'alaykum wa raḥmatūllah wa barakatuh.* The Lord of Heavens is ordering His most beloved one, Sayyidīna Muḥammad ﷺ:

lā nurīdu minkum jaza'an wa lā shukūra.

(Saying), We feed you for the sake of Allāh alone: no reward do we desire from you, nor thanks. *76:9*

O People! Come and listen. Come and listen to what is coming or which thing is coming on people in the coming days and the New Year. There are coming new appearances in this year. We are asking humbly to be granted from our Lord, by the honor of His most honored one, *'amu ibtihāj surūr,* that this year is for benefit, for honor and gives much more satisfaction and carries us from bad situations to good situations.

O People! Say, *Bismillāhi 'r-Raḥmāni 'r-Raḥīm.* You can find your ways. Don't forget to say, *Bismillāhi 'r-Raḥmāni 'r-Raḥīm.*

nasūllaha fanasīyahum

They forgot Allāh, so they were forgotten. *9:67*

O our Salafi *'ulama*! do you think that you are saying this holy verse to your people or to everyone throughout the east and the west? Why do people just fall into worst positions? What is the reason? The Holy Qur'an is explaining and opening meanings to whole servants. That is a heavenly message. When something is coming on people to make them unhappy, they must know what the reason is; *lā tansūha* (do not forget *basmalah*) *nasūllāha wa nasīyahum, "They forgot Allāh and He forgot them."* That is the reason. Why are you not saying this?

O Salafi *'ulama*! You must announce, you must declare that point! That is very important. Every badness or every cursing comes on people for the main reason that they are forgetting their Creator, the Lord of Heavens. When they are forgetting, then cursing coming. If anyone is living with Allāh, then:

lā khawfun 'alayhim wa lā hum yahzanūn

On them shall be no fear, nor shall they grieve. *10: 62*

O People! Come and listen. If you are not coming and listening, heavenly whip is coming on your heads, and more and more troubles are on the way. When one is finishing, another is coming. Last year there was an economic crisis, yes?

O Salafi *'ulama*! Last year an economic crisis descended on the world, what was that, explain to me; who understands Arabic?) Explain to all people, what is the reason that they are falling in that economical crisis? That is written in Holy Qur'an? Don't say, "It is not in the Holy Qur'an," and Allāh Almighty is saying:

wa mā farratna fi 'l-kitābi min shay'in.

Nothing have We omitted from the book. 6:38

This is Arabic or Turkish language? Why are you not saying? They are saying, "We are Salafi *'ulama*!" Then say, "What we said, *Āmantu Billāh.*"

Qur'an 'adhīmu 'sh-shān, in Holy Qur'an you can find an answer for every kind of crisis. If you are asking to get out from crisis, you may say, "What is the Holy Qur'an saying about this?" *Wa mā farratna fi 'l-kitābi min shay'in.* I am asking something and you understand something else, *Māshā'Allāh masriyūn,* and is never understanding Arabic. I am saying, what is the reason that they are falling in crisis and what is the way to save themselves from crisis? Say! Say! I am an old one, must look and listen. I am knowing nothing, but something is coming to my heart. What is the way for saving states from crisis? Say what is *āyatu 'l-karīmah.* What is coming to my heart. Before I said:

mā farratna fi 'l-kitābi min shay.

Everything you ask for, you can find in the Holy Qur'an. 6:38

But letters, big letters, then under it, you may understand. What is the reason? Say! You here are also Arabs. No one knows what is coming to my heart. Who is asking to be saved from crisis? It means that harming people *dhāhiran wa bātinan,* from out-looking and in their inner lives, destroying them. Crisis is destroying Mankind inwardly and outwardly. Inwardly they will be in such a position that they are never going to be happy in their lives, and they are asking to change themselves. Therefore, drinking, drinking, drinking, vodka, whiskey, and champagne. Drinking for what? To change themselves, to take themselves out of miseries. But it is not a real way for saving yourself or for saving all nations from crisis.

Allāh Almighty is giving an answer. When you are falling in such a position that you aren't able to take it away, what is the way? They are making me Say,

nasūllaha fanasīyahum.

They forgot Allāh, so they were forgotten. 9:67

That is the reason for crises. What do you think? One year ago, there was nothing in existence. Suddenly, whole TV centers and radio broadcasts and whole magazine and newspapers saying that a heavy crisis just happened, a big crash. We never thought this would happen. They are asking, "How did this happen?" I am asking, under which one are you living on Earth? Do you know that happened by His holy orders? A crash, opened, cracked, and people falling down. They were never expecting this before. They are so happy. What are they saying? The US announcing throughout the east and west that it just happened, suddenly a crash or crack in the economy and everything falling. What we can do now? I was surprised and saying, what happened? The US was saying $700 billion. That is the reason for the crisis. I am saying $700 billion, with our Salafi *'ulama.* They know so many hundreds of people, only one of them has trillions and trillions of dollars. What happened? The US was claiming, "We are leaders of the whole world." You are the leaders of whole world, and you are falling down with $700 billion?

I may say now, hundreds of people who are rich, their richness is reaching to trillion dollars or even trillion coins, but it is a secret and the government is saying, "What are we going to do?" What are you going to do? Close doors as a merchant who is going to be bankrupt. If you are unable to save people from that crisis, is really a small crisis? But the whole *dunyā* is shaking from east to west and from north to south. For what? $700 billion.

Yā Hu! This big world has 7 billion people. If you are taking one dollar from them, it is going to be 7 billion. If 10, it is going to be 70 billion. If you are taking 100, it is going to be 700 billion. It is too much for a person to give 100 dollars? But the Lord of Heavens teaches people to come to the Right Path, because they are going out of the limits they have been granted. One crisis is happening; if another crisis comes, that means the whole world must fall down and say, "We are finished!" Finished? What is that? But the Lord of Heavens is asking to teach them, to make them understand that the whole worlds, *tasarruf,* organizing is not in your hands but in the hands of heavenly ones.

They are still crying over that *azmatu 'l-iqtasādiyah,* economic crisis. If a second one hitting, "Ohhh, finished." What is the way for saving yourself? That economic crisis is reaching everyone's doors and knowing, "We arrived to you also," poor ones, rich ones, kings, presidents, all of them trembling! That is a heavenly warning.

O People! Keep your good manners, and see what the Lord of Creation created. Why do you think He created you, for collecting money, for collecting land and countries? Did the Lord of Heavens bring you to life for this reason? There is no value in this whole world. No value in Allāh Almighty's Presence. Now they are looking if another crisis coming. They are going to pass away. They are saying, "If a second one hitting, we are going to finish. All of us will fall down." And may come a third one.

Which thing may save you? Say, Salafi *ulama,* what is the way for saving people? What is the Holy Qur'an saying? Say to me; I am asking here. So many people are not answering. What comes to me I shall say to you, because Allāh Almighty is saying:

mā farratna fi 'l-kitābi min shay.

nothing have We omitted from the Book. *6:38*

li kulli da'ain dawā, for every illness there is a medicine. For every problem there is a solution. Allāh Almighty is never leaving people. If giving some troubles for them, He is also giving the solution. The Holy Qur'an is saying *mā farratna fi 'l-kitābi min shay*, for everything, but you are not looking at what the Holy Qur'an is saying.

I am looking, *kullu nāsfī aydihim yatlū Qur'an ʿadhīm yatlū, yatlū* every *nass* (religious text) in their hands *Qur'an ʿadhīm*. I am asking, what you are understanding, O Arabs? Anything? How many times do you make *khatm*, 1000 times and more? What have you learned? Your language is Arabic. What you learned for example, from this economic crisis? What is the Holy Qur'an saying about saving anyone?

O our Listeners! Does anyone know here? I am not playing here and I am not speaking on behalf my ego; it is ashes, finished. There is no hope for me after this age to be a sulṭān or a shaykh al-Islam. Such people are very proud with their imitated titles. No, I am a very, very, very simple *ʿabd*, servant.

O Salafi *ʿulama*! You are not accepting to say, "We are servants." I have never heard from such *muftis* or *sulṭāns* to say, "We are our Lord's servants." They think if they are saying this, their honor will come down. But Allāh Almighty, *man tawaddaʿa lillāh rafaʿahullāh*, "Whoever humbles himself before Allāh, Allāh raises up." But you Ahlu 'l-Hijāz and *ʿulama* Salāfu 's-Sālihīn, you are not saying this in front of all people. I have never heard any sulṭān or any rich one say, "O People! We are servants of our Lord and our ways are to make our Lord happy with us." I am hearing this from no one!

But in 24 hours you are speaking 48 hours. For what is this speaking? Speaking, speaking for what? Why are you not saying, "We are servants of our Lord, and He is putting us on His treasures on this world to do what is best for humanity?" Why are you not saying this? Say! Now that answer is coming from our spiritual centers. It is coming. Who is ordering me to address you, they are now giving the way of saving people physically, economically or in any way that they are falling into troubles. They are falling into endless troubles and sinking in Misery Oceans. Allāh Almighty is saying, *Bismillāhi 'r-Raḥmāni 'r-Raḥīm*, hear and learn! Allāh Almighty is saying, *astaʿidhu billāh*

> *Wa man yattaqillāha yajʿal lahu makhraja, wa yarzuqahu min haythu lā yahtasib.*
> *And for those who fear Allāh, He (ever) prepares a way out and He provides for him from (sources) he never could imagine.* 65:2-3

SadaqAllāhu al-ʿadhīm wa kadhaba 'l-kāfirīn wa kadhaba 'ash-shayatīn... "Allāh told the Truth and the unbelievers and devils called it lies." Anyone saying, "No?" Where is your *taqwa*? You are living in palaces and castles, *tabnūn qusūr*, skyscrapers. Prophet ﷺ was saying fifteen centuries ago, as the sign of the Last Day people will *yatasābiqūn fi 'l-bunyān, wa antum ʿulamā as-salāf, ayyi ʿulama kān yāti jiwāz li yukhrab atrāf baytullāh wa tabni* skylines, competing in building, and you, O scholars of the Salafi, which scholars gave permission to destroy the outer areas of the House of Allāh and to build skylines? Which one is giving that *fatwa*?

Your *sultan*, your king, your *mālik*, which one is going to say? And you Salafi, which *ʿulama* is giving that *fatwa* to build that skyscraper in Mecca? Who is going to say? Where is your *fatwa*? Do you think that Rasūlullāh, when he was saying *yatasābiqūn fi 'l-bunyān,* that it is praising for them? Rasūlullāh ﷺ was happy, or was he saying, "Why you are building these high buildings?" Are you not fearing that if Allāh Almighty orders one angel keeping that area to make an earthquake, very simple, all your buildings coming down with their inside, with people also, to make them down? You are not fearing from Allāh?!

Why are you not saying that is *harām*? After two levels (stories), when a Man is asking to build over two another floor, angels are saying, "O son of Adam, it is not enough for you?" *Inna ardī wāsiyatun,* "Is the bigness of this world not enough for you to build?" And you are building more than 10, 15, 50, 90 floors? Why, are you going to be like Nimrod? Only Nimrod was building so high, saying, "I must get up as much as possible. I must go up to look and see your Lord through angels."

Up to where are you asking to reach, O Man? Are you asking to reach as Nimrod was building high, to look at what is up? Are you not ashamed? Are you not fearing from the warning of the Seal of Prophets ﷺ?

amar bī 'l-maʿrūf wa nahiʿani 'l-munkar.

Enjoin what is right and forbid what is wrong. 31:17

Why are you not saying? You fear *mulūk,* kings, when their lives are like our own, *bayna nafasayn,* "between two breaths." If Allāh Almighty says, "Enter," a breath enters their lungs. If never giving that, they are falling down dead. If anyone is breathing, asking for it to come, but if the Lord of Heavens not giving, then that one is falling. On which thing you are putting *tawwakul,* trust? To your title or your gold or your oil wells? Ha!! *Alḥamdūlillāh,* I am only saying what is coming to my heart, warning people.

O People! Once at the beginning of this century, an earthquake just happened on the 15th of this month in China. Its power was 8.5 (on the Richter Scale). It was falling on people and nearly one million people passed away. *ʿalā tu'min yā ʿibādAllāh li rabbikum innahu qādirun ʿalā kulli shay?* Are you not believing, O servants of Allāh, that your Lord is able to do all things?

> *Innamā amruhu idha arada shayan an yaqūlu lahu kun fa yakūn.*
>
> *Verily, when He intends a thing, His Command is, 'Be', and it is!* *36:82*

You do not believe. If you do not believe, one night may come a *darba,* a heavenly hammer, from above onto your building and to make it Earth. Do you not fear? Fear! You may be *sultan,* you may be *malik,* you may be president, you may be this or that, but you can't carry a certificate from Heavens that nothing is harming you, no. Only Allāh Almighty, if He is protecting, protection. If no one is protecting you, finished.

O People! I am not addressing only Muslims, but I am addressing to whole believers in their religions, people of Christianity or Judaism. They are understanding what the Lord of Heavens is making me address you. Don't think that my tongue is saying a wrong thing when I am sitting here. This is a heavenly warning, or anytime, at any moment you can be taken away.

Look what happened in the US in 1989 (Loma Prieta earthquake); in a second, thousands of people were thrown under their buildings. If the Lord of Heavens is asking to destroy the whole world, He can destroy it in, not minutes or seconds, but less. He may take away from east to west and from north to south! *Illa an yaʿfa ʿan ahādu 'n-nās,* those who will remain are only a handful people that Allāh Almighty is protecting, sheltering them.

O People! This is a heavy warning and this is a very holy month that we are reaching, Muharramu 'l-Haram 1431. Just the Day of Resurrection is approaching! Take yourself away from *dunyā* and *tawajjahu* (turn your spiritual gaze) towards Allāh Almighty if you are asking to be in safety here and Hereafter. If not, no one can save people who are not taking a lesson from a heavenly warning. I am asking forgiveness for me, for you, and for everyone. I hope you are not thinking this declaration is from myself; it is not. It is a heavenly declaration and must be suitable to the Holy Qur'an, the Bible, the Old Testament, the New Testament, and Psalms.

O our Lord! For the honor of Your best one, most holy one, most glorified servant, Sayyidīna Muḥammad ﷺ, save ourselves send us someone from Your special servants to take ourselves from the wrong way to the Right Path!

May Allāh forgive us, for the honor of the most beloved one. O our Lord, *astaghfirullāh.* The angels looking at who is hearing and who, out of them, leaving to hear such a declaration. Beware, O People! If something is coming as a punishment, who that is for? May Allāh forgive us and save ourselves from the badness of our egos for the honor of the most honored one.

O People! Try to do your best. That is only what the Lord of Heavens is asking from you, from every kind of religious people who are claiming, "We are Christian, we are Jewish, we are Muslims," the Lord of Heavens is looking to you. Whatever you are doing, say, "O our Lord, we are trying to do our best." Then you will be saved here and Hereafter.

O Salafi *'ulama*! Don't be angry with me, because anger harms you and it is never harming me. Look! *Istaqim*! *Qul āmantu billāh thumma ' staqim,* "Stand up for truth! Say, 'I put my trust in Allāh, then stand forth for truth!'" This is the last advice for all nations.

May Allāh ﷻ forgive us.

Fātiḥah.

"O My Lord, I Tried to Know Your Orders"

Aʿūdhu billāhi min ash-Shaytāni 'r-rajīm. Biṣmillāhi 'r-Raḥmāni 'r-Raḥīm. Dastūr, yā Sayyidī. Madad, yā rijālAllāh!

As-salāmu *ʿalaykum yā ʿibādAllāh,* the servants of our Lord, Allāh Almighty. O our Lord! Forgive us, help us, bless us. *Alfu, alfu salāt, alfu, alfu salām ʿalā Sayyidi 'l-Awwalīn wa 'l-Ākhirīn.*

We are saying, *aʿūdhu billāhi min ash-Shaytāni 'r-rajīm. Bismillāhi 'r-Raḥmāni 'r-Raḥīm.* If you are asking for a connection with heavenly levels, you must say *aʿūdhu billāhi min ash-Shaytāni 'r-rajīm* and Shaytān is just kicked out. And we are saying, *Bismillāhi 'r-Raḥmāni 'r-Raḥīm,* and angels saying, "Welcome to you, welcome to you, our Lord's servant."

We know nothing. We are only depending on what our Grandshaykh is putting in my heart and speaking. I am not claiming that I am knowing something. Everyone is knowing more than me and according to your knowledge you will be judged.

"O My servant! Come and say, what you learned in your whole life?" "I learned this and that, this and that." And as you learned, you lived. You were making just straight on that way? You learned but were not keeping what you learned. What you must learn? *Madad yā Sulṭān al-Awlīyā, madad yā RijālAllāh.* What you are going to learn, when He, Almighty asking? We must know what we learned and for what we learned it.

"I learned to be driver. I learned to know how to fly planes. I learned to be a computer engineer. I learned to build concrete buildings. I learned how to make a car. I learned baking. I learned important things. I learned to be shepherd."

You, what you learned?

"I was such a person never learning, but I am putting on my chest and behind me, 'political person,' you know? Because I was first-class person and I just fought against monarchies and coming on their thrones to make my ego happy and to be so proud."

So many kinds of learning. If the Lord of Heavens is asking, "I don't know how many people may say, 'I tried to know Your orders'; I learned how I can keep my ego from evils; I learned how people can save themselves from devils." You may ask, "What is it, devils?" Devils are cheating ones, O People. Cheating people. Cheaters. Perhaps from billions, you may take a handful of people who were trying to learn about their Lord. Leave about their Lord, but they were asking to know what are the rights of their Creator. Now people are foolish ones. If you are asking, "How you are in existence?" he is saying, "My dad through my mom creating me." Your "Creator" is your mom and dad? *Hāsha*! *Ptuu* (spit)! No one saying, "My Lord created me." And what was your mission when you know Who created you? Then you learned what was your mission?

This is for all Mankind now that they may be listening throughout east and west. *Āyatul karīmah.*

thumma latus'alunna yawmaidhin ʿani 'n-naʿīm.

Then, shall you be questioned that Day, about the joy (you indulged in). 102:8

O our Salafi *ʿulama*! what you are saying? You are Arabs and you know too much; claiming, but you are never saying. Except Arabs, they understand. I am asking to you, what Allāh Almighty saying? *Astaʿidhu billāh,* tell me, *waqifūhum,* "Make them stop!" *Qif*! Stop! For what? *Innahum mas'ūlūn*. Arabs, where are Arabs? But I am saying to those proud *ʿulama*, Salafis or *khalafis*!

Waqifūhum innahum mas'ūlūn.

But stop them, for they must be asked. 37:24

Why you are not saying Hanbali, Shafiʿi or Maliki *ʿulama*? What means *salaf*? *Salaf,* you may understand as just passed away, from the time of Adam up to today. You are representing those people? Why you are saying (you are) "Salafi"? Do you think you know what Jesus Christ ﷺ was teaching *hawāriyyūn*, his disciples?

Today is a new beginning of the year 1431, and the Lord of Heavens is not happy with us because all of us are disobedient servants! You can't find a handful of obedient servants. Therefore, just moved heavenly anger and approaching. I don't know what is going to happen in this holy month, Muharramu 'l-*Harām*. Allāh Almighty was reaching to His prophets (to protect them) when *shayatīn* and their followers disturbing and rushing on them for killing them. And they were asking, "O our Lord! Reach to Your weak servants. Disobedient servants are rushing on us, asking to take ourselves away and to make this globe only for *shaytans*, not to be for

Allāh." Their aim, their last target and hope, is to make this whole world *lā dīni,* without any religion!

But a heavenly anger is ready to come on their heads! I am running away to Allāh Almighty because I am not happy with my ego. If anyone is happy with their ego, they are not happy with Allāh, because first fighter according to the Lord of Heavens, was our ego. Our ego never going to be an obedient one. Therefore, I am saying when the Lord of Heavens is asking, "What you learned about Me? And then, what you learned about My rights on you, as I am Creator; what were My rights on My servants, you learned it?"

"No, we were secular ones"

"Take them away (from My Presence)!"

Astaghfirullāh, Astaghfirullāh, Astaghfirullāh.

I heard in Madinatu 'l-Munawwara when that eclipse happening a secret sound saying, *astaghfirullāh, astaghfirullāh, astaghfirullāh, astaghfirullāh,* "O Allāh, forgive me." O People! Say *astaghfirullāh.* The Seal of Prophets ﷺ was saying, "I am saying *astaghfirullāh* daily, 70 times." If he is saying it 70 times, for us 70 million is not enough!

You can look and see in the faces of a very few people, a clean face, brightened face, enlightened face. Very, very, very few! (Mawlana mimics as if grooming in mirror.) That man, looking very handsome and ladies at every foot, they are taking and looking. (Laughter) So many ones that they are using so many cosmetics. Coming from them very bad-smelling. Therefore, they are trying to cover that smelling from themselves by using cosmetics.

Saḥābah of the Seal of Prophets ﷺ were dressing one shirt that you can't know if it was white or black. They had no water for washing and if washing one, they must sit naked waiting for it to dry. Therefore, they are using this for life and my grandshaykh was saying to me, "O Nazim Effendi, their clothes you can't differentiate if it is white or black, but if you are smelling, it is smelling of best perfume of roses."

Prophet's ﷺ command was saying, *tāhiru turūqu 'l-Qur'an,* "Purify the pathways of Qur'an." Keep clean. It is the way of *imān,* the way of *dhikr,* the way of life. Every *Saḥābah* ؓ, their breathings just so beautiful smelling, because they were clean, they were following holy commands of Allāh Almighty, *tāhiru turūqu 'l-Qur'an.* May Allāh ﷻ forgive us.

O People! People are on the wrong way and therefore, crisis climbing. Not coming down, but day-by-day getting more and more and more until they are coming to the way of Paradise. If not, they will be taken away! That is, all nations now, looking about expected huge events, mentioned in *ḥadīth sharīf, al-marhamatu 'l-kubra*. Beware, O People! Hear, listen and obey. The Lord of Heavens is asking that knowledge: what you learned about your Creator and what you learned about your Lords' rights, how you are doing for His rights? Learn this, as no one is learning; everyone trying to learn about this *dunyā*! Even the Muslim world is trying to be westernized...

May Allāh forgive me, and forgive you. We are hoping in this holy month for heavenly help and support for weak servants. We are not claiming we are doing any servanthood but we are asking for forgiveness. Forgive us, O our Lord, for the honor of Your most honored servant, Sayyidīna Muḥammad ﷺ.

May Allāh ﷻ forgive us.

Fātiḥah.

Evolutionism versus Perfect Creation

Aʿūdhu billāhi min ash-Shayṭāni 'r-rajīm. Biṣmillāhi 'r-Raḥmāni 'r-Raḥīm. Dastūr, yā Sayyidī. Madad, yā rijālAllāh!

Lā ilāha illa-Llāh, lā ilāha illa-Llāh, lā ilāha illa-Llāh Muḥammadun Rasūlullāh Dastūr yā RijālAllāh. As-salāmu ʿalaykum yā ʿibādAllāh.

Don't be *ʿabdu nafsak*, dirtiest one is that one who going to be a slave of his ego; dirtiest one and thrown away from heavenly stations. Therefore, beware on your egos; it is equal to beware of Shaytān. You are listeners, yes, we must listen.

O our master, who is controlling everything throughout east and west, from north to south, on skies and under oceans! You must know that there can't be two *irādah,* wills, on one planet. Who may show his will and may do according to his will, not anyone else. That is important. That is a very important point. Now we are trying to understand something from our grandshaykh, who is *quṭb fī 'd-dunyā, quṭb* for this world.

You must believe, O all *ʿulama,* who are claiming they are *ʿulama.* I'm not addressing only Salafi *ʿulama,* but all *ʿulama* from east to west who are saying they are learned people. You may say that, "I am a learned one, *ʿalim.* I am knowing so many holy verses in Holy Qur'an and I know also thousands of *ḥadīth,* knowledge that just arrived to us from Heavens through heavenly messengers." Are you claiming that your whole knowledge keeping in your memory or in your heart?

You know to a limit, but beyond that limit do you know? Don't say, "I am an *ʿalim* (scholar)," but say, "I am *tālib* (student), I am asking to learn." And that is high honor for Mankind, to learn from holy knowledge. Don't think that what is on Earth, so many animals in the animal world, so many plants in the plants world, it is only that one or it is enough for you. Yes, all of them signifying the existence for a creature. If there is no Creator, there will be no creatures, because it never happened that a creature brings itself in existence by itself. Who may claim this?

But so many foolish ones say Man descended from apes. What is your evidence? And is it so shining evidence they are using it for their knowledge to say that Man came from apes? Any evidence? No evidence. But they are saying about their creation that, "This is our creation, that we are coming into existence from nothing in existence and being something." But they are not ashaming to say, "We are coming from apes in existence." Not ashaming and not believing also!

This is a big blame from those people also, who are claiming they are coming from apes. This is your honor? That is an honor to say this and to be happy? Yes, you are apes! Oh, if it was what you are saying, you will be dust finally and you are not calling for a judgment and the Lord of Heavens giving animals. Also coming on the Day of Judgment and saying turn back as you were, turn back to your origin. What was their origin? It was dust!

They are going to their origins, but can you, Man, come and say how you are claiming that if are coming from apes? And apes, on the Day of Resurrection, are going to turn back to their real being that was dust, going to be dust. But you are here now, I'm not commanding to your physical being, "turn back to be dust," no. Your physical being going to be on same creation of, *lahm*, flesh and bones.

But you have been granted something more, that giving to be an honor. They have been granted that grant. They are taken from Earth and sending back to their real beings. But you, you were created, the Creator created you as He likes and you were only a Man's structure, or Man's shape, nothing. You were just bones and flesh, first creating you from Earth and you were a shape just appeared as a Man, but no action in yourself, no. You were only like a dead body. Everything okay, as a person just fell into sea and getting out and putting in a place. You are looking, that is a Man and we are looking that nothing is absent from this body and they are saying coming from apes! If his life coming from apes, you may bring an ape to give what it has to that drowned body to make it up, as sometimes there are two batteries and they are saying this one is empty not working; you must bring another battery that is working to bring from its charger to that one that is finished.

Do you see what was in it? Do you see what it lost or what was that full battery? They are saying one working but we must bring this one, to bring something from it. Anyone explaining? No. We are putting two wires and leaving and saying now it is okay, just full and charged, yes. And animals that they are claiming to be the ancestors of Mankind, what they were carrying from secrets that giving to them to stand up and to do so many things, unless they are apes? How happening? But people are not thinking, they are not thinking anything. That is a principle that putting empty battery with full battery, and no one seeing finished this one, and what that another one giving to it. Never you can see.

Therefore, they are foolish and ignorant to believe that Man came from apes. What are apes giving to a man? Who is giving must be much more powerful. How apes are still on their level but is Man standing up, living, making, building, destroying, killing everything? Apes are apes! (laughter) But people think they are superior ones, claiming this because who said? One priest said this and you are believing him and denying 124,000 holy ones who say, "Your Lord created you, and before that your physical being had no life in it."

After that, Allāh Almighty ordered the soul, it is a being or a creation, but no one knows its identity. It was a dead body and then something entered it and first he was moving, his eyes opening and looking. Then that secret power made the eyes of that new creation to see, and that power ran through that shape, and the Lord of Heavens created Man from earth, but that earth was beginning to move! How it can be? That secret point granted from the Lord of Heavens to Man made Man's creation on the top point. Others are created but they haven't been granted a secret power to think, to know and to do!

But those who are claiming they are professors really know nothing because no one knows Man's creation except their Creator. Don't make your level on or below the level of animals! Where is your honor? As being from human nature, how you can say apes are on the same level with Man? Man has so many specialities that makes it on a higher level from animals! Who doesn't have something can't give it, and animals don't have the speciality of Mankind!

O professors, O scientists, O liars, O *shaytans* who are claiming Man came from apes! Darwin said this, and you are not believing the declaration of 124,000 special beings, but believing a crazy one. How? First there is a rule in nature that something that appears once may appear several times or endlessly. Man is most honored one in existence on this world. How you are claiming Man came from apes? Who accepts that his grandfather was an ape but he came as a man? If your grandfather was an ape, he was speaking? He was making something? He learned something? No!

How you are saying you came from something that does not have the attributes granted to Man? Why you are claiming and making so much nonsense?! You are not ashaming to say this? From where apes and cats came? Cats are very proud ones because they are saying, "Our uncle is a lion," and saying *meoww, meowww*! They are so important ones, for what? Someone saying to them, "If your uncle accepting you to be its child from its generation, from where you are coming to me? I am lion! When I roar, the whole jungle trembles, so what you are saying, '*meowww*'? Who is listening to that from you? I am the king of jungles, and there is no relation between lions and cats!" Even cats look like lions, but small size. We are thinking that dogs not claiming to say, "Our ancestors were wolves," and wolves saying, "We are so proud that our grandfather was apes," and apes very angry, saying, "Who are you to say you are a lion from my generation? Go away or I will kill you!!"

Another and another, so many kinds of Creation, everyone claiming and looking at themselves as the best creatures. They are not happy saying, "Cats come from lions." Jaguars saying, "My grandfather was the tiger." Tiger is saying, "Who are you to be my grandson? Go away!" No one asking to be like another creature, but Mankind is so foolish, in such a mental house, never getting out with such a foolish ideas, bringing such a foolish ones to make the understanding of Mankind in such a way that not to say our Creator created us as humans!

Donkey saying, "I am thankful to my Lord, Who created me." So many saying that we are coming from this or from that academies. I am saying that if coming, make what donkey making *"hee haw hee haw*!" Make it, make how monkeys are shouting! I am asking those people who are believing their ancestors were apes, make like it and look its face and your face in mirror, how you are claiming this? And I'm sorry that in the whole world, who is teaching that they are coming from apes, they should go not to Paradise, they are not smelling even its beautiful smell!

Use your mind and try to know Who created you and for what He created you, and which thing your Lord asks you to do! You are running after Shaytān and Shaytān carries people to the Fire! Their life here is in miseries and sufferings and Next-World fire awaits them! May Allāh forgive us!

It is such dangerous claiming and very shameful for Man to come from his high level to dirtiest level of animals! How they are doing this as a knowledge? Such things making the Lord of Heavens to be angry for them and opening the door of technology to kill, to destroy each other's cities and countries. That is the Lord's punishment for those who are following Shaytān and its representatives! And then you are claiming, "Holy Qur'an says this," and, "We are not believing this; we are such new ones, learning new knowledge!" What is your knowledge? Try to learn Holy Qur'an! Allāh Almighty sending Holy Qur'an for you to learn about Who created you! Without learning this, you are on the wrong way! If you don't know about yourself and what you have been created from, you are on the wrong way! You must learn true way, O Mankind, or heavenly punishment coming on you daily and nightly.

May Allāh forgive us and bless us for the honor of the most honored one in His Divine Presence, Sayyidīna Muḥammad ﷺ. This is for those who understand their positions, heavenly and earthly! (Mawlana sings.) That singing gives some spirituality to the hearts of people! May Allāh ﷻ forgive us. *Fatihah.*

They are making themselves such creatures that they are always asking to be friendly with an ox. They are very happy to be with oxen or donkeys, but they are under their tail coming there making shower also. (Mawlana laughs.) They are very clean ones because they are asking several times daily to make a shower, because they are very friendly with cows and sitting behind cows and cows making showers, *shooooooo.* (laughter) Now so many people are leaving Holy Qur'an and following Darwin. Their example just this sitting there then suddenly *shooooooo*, shower for us!

O our Listeners! How are you? May laugh His Holiness, the Pope, may laugh His Holiness (the) Patriarch, may laugh for this even kings, Muslim kings and Muslim presidents may laugh for this, Jewish rabbis also are so happy with what we are saying. Only you must clean yourselves, O Muslims. Only clean ones going to enter Paradise, and dirty ones will not.

May Allāh ﷻ forgive us. Good night this night, for new understanding because New Year coming, and people preparing themselves for Christmas and such things. Therefore, this is a preparation for their mindly productions.

May Allāh ﷻ forgive us.

Fātiḥah.

Be Clean and Come to the Lord!

Aʿūdhu billāhi min ash-Shaytāni 'r-rajīm. Bismillāhi 'r-Raḥmāni 'r-Raḥīm. Dastūr, yā Sayyidī. Madad, yā rijālAllāh!

D*astūr yā Sayyidī, madad. Allāhu Akbar, Allāhu Akbar, lā ilāha illa-Llāh Allāhu Akbar Allāhu Akbar wa lillāhi 'l-ḥamd*! He is the Lord of all creatures. He is the Creator, not anyone else! And all Creation just coming in existence for the honor of His most honored and beloved and glorified servant, Sayyidīna Muḥammad ﷺ. O our Lord, for his honor forgive us, and for his honor grant us from Your endless blessings.

O our master, master of this world, that he is appointed from Heavens for controlling everything and preparing everything for our Lord's servants, may Allāh bless him and give him much more lights and glory!

O our Listeners! We are saying *as-salāmu 'alaykum,* all Mankind! Hear and listen and obey. That is our *wasīya,* advice to everyone. First, my advice to my ego. We must try to order our egos. If a person not going to be able to order his ego, no value for that person here or Hereafter.

O our Listeners! O Mankind! We are all Mankind, but we have been honored by the Lord of Creation to be His special servants. That means to be His deputies. Deputies can't do anything by themselves, but they will be under holy command of Heavens so that they can do what it is asked from them and (spread the message), "O Mankind! Hear and listen and obey!" Every time we must say this:

wa tawāsaw bī 'l-haqq.

And (join together) in the mutual teaching of Truth. 103:3

Allāh Almighty is saying that for those Who is asking to save themselves and also everyone. Who is asking to save himself or herself and also to save all creatures on this planet, one of them just honored on this planet. Mankind has been honored in the Heavens. And countless creatures in Creation of the Creator going to be with us on this planet, but honor only given for Mankind because they are deputies for their Creator.

O our Lord! Give us something for understanding. Allāh ﷻ says, "I granted to you, but you are running after your egos."

O Mankind, what the Lord of Heavens granted to you, that heavenly grant, you are not using for your Creator, Who honored you to be His deputies. When you are using what you have been granted by Allāh Almighty for yourself, your dirty egos and egoist demands, then your high value coming down! When a person's value falling from Heavens to Earth, he lost all value that granted by Allāh Almighty for them, finished! There is a fruit, *mushmush*, apricot, as long as keeping itself on its position on branch, it is so good. As long as tree keeping that, it is okay; but if tree going to tire from it and leaving, coming on Earth, finished!

O People! Keep your positions, not to fall from Heavens on Earth. Who is on Heavens, his value just excellent. If falling down, then going to be no value and no way. Taking that apricot that just becoming dirty, taking and eating? No. That is important. Try to be clean to the end of your life and the One Who granted to you that cleanliness, taking you clean and putting you on a clean level, and you will be respected one! But who are not looking for their positions, and leaving themselves to fall on Earth, that bush taking it away.

O People! Try to be clean ones from every dirtiness on this planet. Try to be clean for whole life so that when the Angel of Death comes and asks, "Give what is granted to you from the Lord of Heavens, give it to me." Looking if it is clean, then just taken to the level of honor, the level of holiness, the level of lights, the level of oceans. Thank you! Why you are losing level of honor, making every dirtiness here in this short time. Why you are not keeping yourself clean, O Mankind? Therefore, every prophet, peace be upon them, and the Seal of Prophets ﷺ was saying, "Believers must be clean. Unbelievers, they are not clean ones." What we must do? How we can do? What have we been granted from our Lord to ourselves? How we can deal with ourselves and how we are going to deal with our Creator? That is knowledge, *'ilmun nafi'ah.* That knowledge is giving you benefit because that knowledge keeping you clean. If not that knowledge, they are always in dirtiness.

The Seal of Prophets, peace be upon him, was saying, "Cleanliness is *imān.*" If a person not going to be clean, no belief in himself, he is not believing for his Creator and His holy commands. We must learn this. Therefore, Allāh Almighty ordering to His most beloved one to teach people, "Be clean." Try to be clean. Cleanliness is not cleanliness of our suits or our clothes, but inside you must be clean. (Allāh Almighty is saying,) "Don't come to Me dirty. Who is coming dirty, he is not accepted!" Anyone asking to be acceptable in Heavens must be clean, as believers never coming for worshipping without ablution, or without shower. Therefore, main point for everyone to learn in his life is to be clean, and when they are clean, they must keep their Lord's most high glorifying. You must try that He grants to you heavenly glorifying. Who is not thinking on it, they are not granted any grant here or Hereafter. They will be dirty ones and dirty ones are outside, take them to be clean. Where? In fire, they may be clean there, O our Lord!

O People! Listen and obey, clean your ears for listening because our ears, our hearing, full with *shaytanic* singings and *shaytanic* speakings and *shaytanic* orders. It is not for you! O People! You must try to be clean ones. Don't think that to be doctors, scientists, PhDs, academics, or to be in high positions for your learned matters is making you clean! It is never giving any benefit to you, but if you are asking benefit for future life, here and Hereafter, then you must be clean ones. Therefore, coming all prophets, particularly the Seal of Prophets, ordering to be, clean, clean, clean!

Clean in what you are dressing, eating and learning. If you are giving to you cleanliness, okay. If not, you will be in a well filled with dirtiness. We reached the Last Days for the life of Mankind, according to holy knowledge that granted to prophets. You can't know this from new books. They never showing or teaching you what is real knowledge that is making you to be clean ones. So many professors, so many learned people, so many doctors, so many academic peoples, only their titles something but their inner position is so dirty! If anyone's thinking is dirty, that means his production is dirty. That person is going to be like the WC (bathroom) or sewage channels. If a person not giving to you a cleanliness, that person like the WC. Who running in the WC? Rats. They are very happy to go in sewage channels, and they are saying we are making shower also, going freely throughout east and west, running, jumping, eating. We just asking to reach our last target. We reached there and we never asking anything beyond this. It is perfect target also for Man, to be able to think on it.

"What you are saying, to come out? We are finding everything in sewage channels. Look our bodies are so weak ones."

And those rats saying, "Some Man may hunt you and making you barbecue. Beware, O our friends, run away from Mankind. If they are hunting you in fire you will be so tasteful meals for Mankind, run away! Don't show yourselves, keep yourselves, hide yourselves because they are running after you and we are here so happy. If we are unhappy we may call them, we may do weekly meeting making advertisement, 'O People! who asking a high life, they must join our group. We may take you to an unexpected high life that Mankind they can't dream or imagine our lives here.'"

Some of them asking for rats, "Who teaching you?" "Our teacher asking to teach you but you are escaping from it. Our teacher is Shaytān, Diabolo. Our teacher, teaching us also to call everyone outside to come and to enter."

Glory to Allāh Almighty! Now everywhere, particularly at nighttime, east and west, people running into sewage channels. "O Shaykh, what about preparing us for Christmas? Christmas enjoyment; we were hoping and wishing to be every night Christmas, every day to be Christmas!"

(Rats saying:) "But those foolish Mankind not following us and making this big feast, they are making only once annually because no-mind, Mankind. If they are like us they are understanding, because we are experts at such parties and we are doing parties that Mankind making it only once yearly, but we are preparing every night this feast and enjoyment. Therefore, we are calling them, 'Come, O Mankind, to be with us.'"

That is Shaytān's declaration. Really Shaytān is teaching Mankind, "Come and join everyone Christmas day or night because it is so pleasure in it and you must come. You must try not to only do once yearly, but every night you must do this, come with us, to be like us!"

"I'm the chief of rats, so learned one, because our ancestors also they are teaching me and I am teaching to new ones for tasting a real taste and to be there every night, Christmas night, everyday Christmas day but they are not following us because they are saying, 'O we prepared some money only for one night. How we will be every night in sewage channel?' And that rat saying, "look you are dressing anything? ....take all clothes and daily seven times and nightly 10 times, go in it and get out, go in it and get out." Then what about our clothes?" "You are going after a while feathers coming out and .....no need for clothes.........??...no government, no national military, no schools, no factories, no government officials, no, come with us. Try to be with us here, free, never-ending enjoyment, never-ending eating and drinking in sewage channels."

That is the meaning that Shaytān making people *targhīb*, to encourage them, "Leave everything and come and enjoy yourself." That is top point of Shaytān's training for Mankind, "Leave everything and follow us."

O our Listeners! As all prophets saying, that is going to be the end of this world. Dajjal, the Antichrist, coming and saying, "No work, no national service, nothing. Come with me and you can find what you are asking." Finally that Antichrist calling people and cheating them; now Antichrist has representatives throughout the east and west and everywhere you can find people of foolish minds saying, everyday and every night, "No working and..."

O our Lord! Please forgive us and send us someone to clean us and to teach us what heavenly ones asking to be for us. Heavens asking, "O My servants, try to be clean ones," and Shaytān and its rats saying, "Come with us, enjoy yourself." What is happening now, every kind of dirtiness in youngsters running, running, running, making them to dirtiness that if it is opening, no one living from its bad smelling!

O People! O our Listeners! The Lord of Heavens is calling you, me and everyone, "Be clean and come to Me." And cleanliness being in your mind, body, and hearts. "Be clean and come to Me! If you are not clean, you are never coming in My Heavenly Presence." prophets calling to cleanliness and Shaytān calling people to dirtiness. You are between two ways, one showing to cleanliness, second showing people the way of dirtiness.

This is whole world, they are saying, "happy, modern life." What happy, modern life? They never asking heavenly cleanliness. People left worshiping, left their holy places, their mosques, temples, cathedrals and also after that there is for kings, buildings. They never asking. Therefore, people now they are saying, "What we can do in this bad economical crisis?" First clean yourself, then that cleanliness taking you out from dirtiness, but they are not coming. They are only making *shikwah,* complaining. Be clean and you will be saved here and Hereafter from every dirtiness, from every badness, every cruelty and every dirty thing but people never hearing. They are saying, 'modern life.' What is modern life? To live as rats? No differentiation between clean and dirty? That is modern life? They never liked the life of people who were living before this period of time. Everyone was trying to keep themselves clean and to be their Lords' servants, but now they lost their Creator and saying, 'No we must eat drink and enjoy.'

May Allāh ﷻ forgive us.

O People! Be clean, save yourself! If you are not going to be clean, no safety for you here or Hereafter and you will be unhappy with such people. I am sorry to say Muslim world is also following western life. And I'm surprised we have *'ulama* not saying anything, never saying and they are fearing from whom? They are not fearing from Allāh but they are fearing from their children, their families, because they taught them in such institutes or universities. They are teaching their children and their children never listening to them. Even the sons of kings, queens, no one listening to them. Muslim world also, their sons and daughters looking, to reach the night of Christmas. What is your relationship with Christmas, O Muslim community? O Muslims! Why you are asking that? Not shaming from Allāh Almighty to follow Shaytān and not listening to Allāh? May come a heavenly punishment in this year that you will be regretting in the whole year.

O People! Beware of Shaytān. If not, heavenly punishment is ready this year. It is a heavy year and it is very terrible events, like camel caravan following people one-after-one! Beware of Shaytān, leave Christmas. Leave western people to follow Christmas. Muslims, follow the way of the Lord of Heavens, so you will be happy here and Hereafter. May Allāh forgive us!

Allāh Allāh, Allāh Allāh, Allāh Allāh, ʿAzīz Allāh
Allāh Allāh, Allāh Allāh, Allāh Allāh, Karīm Allāh
Allāh Allāh, Allāh Allāh, Allāh Allāh, SubḥānAllāh
Allāh Allāh, Allāh Allāh, Allāh Allāh, Sulṭān Allāh

May Allāh Almighty save us from dirtiness, make us clean ones to be in His Divine Presence.

May Allāh ﷻ forgive us.

Fātiḥah.

Ask from Those with Goodness in Their Faces

A'ūdhu billāhi min ash-Shaytāni 'r-rajīm. Bişmillāhi 'r-Raḥmāni 'r-Raḥīm. Dastūr, yā Sayyidī. Madad, yā rijālAllāh!

Madad, lā ilāha illa-Llāh, lā ilāha illa-Llāh, lā ilāha illa-Llāh Muḥammadun Rasūlullāh 'alayhi salātullāh wa salām. Thumma as-salāmu 'alayk Yā Sāhib al-Waqt, thumma as-salāmu 'alayk Yā Sulṭān al-Awlīyā, thumma as-salātu wa 's-salāmu 'alayk Yā Quṭb az-Zamān.

We are saying, *a'ūdhu billāhi min ash-Shaytāni 'r-rajīm. Bismillāhi 'r-Raḥmāni 'r-Raḥīm. Shukr Yā Rabbī,* all thanks and all praising and all glorifying for You, O our Lord, O our Creator.

We are saying, *A'ūdhu billāhi min ash-Shaytāni 'r-rajīm. Bismillāhi 'r-Raḥmāni 'r-Raḥīm.* Shaytān is most jealous one in Creation and everyone that are also jealous belonging to Shaytān. We are asking protection from Shaytān and its followers. Hundreds and thousands and millions from people, Shaytān graduating them. Giving them, "That is your certificate, now you are just on my footsteps and you are number one and I am so proud that I am graduating you as being most jealous one." Shaytān making, "O my real follower."

May Allāh protect us, *yā Rabb, yā Rabb.* Our egos belong to Shaytān. Therefore, jealous, angry, stubborn people belong to Shaytān, graduated from its academy, and not only one academy, because all followers of Shaytān are very anxious to have a certificate from *shaytanic* academies.

One asking me, "How many academies, O Shaykh," I say 'I don't know, ask stubborn people. *Kibr,* arrogance, that one also from *shaytanic* attributes, arrogance, I never heard such a foolish word. *Kibr,* to see himself over the level of everyone. *Kibr, hasad,* jealous and stubborn also, and anger. These four worst *khisāl,* attributes, all belong to Shaytān. Whom he has one of them, that one must follow Shaytān. Can't enter to Paradise and can't pass over the bridge, *sirāt* over fire, must fall down.

Therefore, all prophets coming for cleaning Man from *shaytanic* attributes. Every prophet coming, first, proud people saying, "Who are you? We are not following you because you look like nothing! We are not seeing you on our level. Who are you to say you are giving declarations from Heavens that 'I am coming to teach you?' Who are you?" They are such proud ones. Pride prevents people from following a heavenly messenger. The worst characteristics of Man are to be proud, stubborn, jealous or angry. Most tribes are filled with very angry people. That is not a beautiful or lovely characteristic for Mankind. Until you are changing these four, you can't enter Paradise. These four characteristics belong to Shaytān. When Allāh Almighty ordered His angels, "Bow to Adam" (Mawlana bows), all angels bowed, and only Shaytān was standing.

Allāh Almighty never addressed such a dirty one! But on behalf of the first level of Heavens, an angel said, "Why you are not making *sajdah*?" Allāh Almighty never going to address such a dirty and ugly creature. His form just changed also. When through himself his dirty position, dirty being appearing, quickly Shaytān's form changed also and going to be in such an ugly form; angels just dressed Shaytān. If you are looking even one moment, your inside going to be just mixing, everything.

O People! *As-salāmu 'alaykum.* Here, don't look there. Look to me, you are seeing me but I must see you also from east to west. The holy command of the Lord of Heavens just changed when Shaytān was disobedient, and he looks like a most ugly one. If you are looking at a person and his looking is ugly, you must understand that something is wrong with that person. Yes,

O our respected *'ulama* from every kind, particularly Salafi *'ulama.* Look in the mirror. If you are seeing yourself handsome, you must fall to *sajdah* that, "I have a heavenly light on my face; therefore, I am a handsome creature." If you are looking and seeing, (Mawlana frowns) "That is myself? I didn't think I was such an ugly one," then put on your face a mask and after tomorrow night, our Christian brothers are using artificial masks on their faces for covering their ugliness.

If you are heavenly ones, your personality is just stamped on your face; a follower of the Lord of Heavens. Or you are a follower of Shaytān and there is a *shaytānic* stamp on your face. O our important, important, important *'ulama*, Salafi *'ulama*, you must know this! What you are saying now? There is one *ḥadīth sharīf* in which the Seal of Prophets ﷺ was saying. His knowledge is like an ocean and from that ocean you may take meanings from that ocean endlessly. *Ḥadīth an-Nabawī ash-sharīf* where the Holy Prophet ﷺ was never speaking for himself; he was speaking on behalf of his Lord because he is *tarjumān*, more than translator, he is representing his Lord.

Therefore, every word that the Seal of Prophets says, shows a shining on their faces. There is one *ḥadīth*, when a person says to you, O Salafi *'ulama* and others, you must remember. You are saying *tad'aī* (claiming). You are Arab and not understanding *tad'aī*? when you are remembering one thing and beyond it you may find on the same level so many things. From one to second to third, jumping and coming to you. What Prophet ﷺ is saying, this very important *ḥadīth sharīf*. It is good, *yalīq*, a writing by golden letters that *ḥadīthu 'sh-sharīf*. It is a balance for Mankind, never changed.

What is that *ḥadīth sharīf*, Shaykh al-Azhar? Say! Remembering or not? You must remember. They are saying to my heart and I am speaking to you: *qāla 'alayhi 's-salātu wa 's-salām, utlubu 'l-ma'rūf 'inda hisani 'l-wujūh.* Is this Arabic or Turkish? Always your faces like this, never smiling to anyone! Always anger on your faces and that anger giving you ugliness. Be as Prophet ﷺ saying, *utlubu 'l-ma'rūf inda hisāni 'l-wujūh.* Therefore, I am asking to reach to 'AbdAllāh, King of Hijāz, because his face is so lovely!

Sometime I am intending to go to him and say, "O Your Majesty, your face is so handsome and I am coming, according to *wasīyatu 'r-Rasūl,* the Prophet's advice, and asking for one million *riyals*; not one billion, but one million, and it doesn't matter because you are so handsome! Really, I am saying how many kings coming through more than His Majesty King 'AbdAllāh, *ayyadahullāh,* may Allāh support him. Then I am looking and my heart opening. Therefore, it is an unchangeable balance: if you are asking for some *ma'rūf,* goodness from a person, look to his face. *Ana 'arabiyyatī qalīl jiddan lākin utlub al-khayr 'inda wujūhu'l-ihsān* (My Arabic is little but I know that saying, "Seek goodness from those possessing good faces.")

What about Salafi *'ulama* ? If his face is lovely, handsome, say, "Please, I am asking for Your Majesty's generosity, one million dollars."

Who gave you that wealth? Allah ﷻ gave you. What did *Rasūlullāh* ﷺ say?

> *Anfiq bilā lā wa lā takhāf man dhil 'arshi iqlāla.*
>
> *Give without (saying) 'no' and do not fear humiliation from Lord of the Throne.*

Sayyidīna 'Uthman ؓ was the wealthiest in the time of Prophet ﷺ. There is no comparison between us and between the Prince of the Believers. Whereas he was giving out two shawls full of *dinars,* we need to distribute the same, to imitate the Rightly Guided Caliphs.

"Ask for favors from those with good-looking faces."

Spend a lot and do not fear humiliation from the Lord of the Throne. The king of Hijāz has instead of *dinars,* diamonds. If he filled two bags with diamonds or red gold, it would not affect his treasure. Ask from His Highness and may Allāh give him more from His bounty. The fourth can fill up with sterling pounds then the fifth with gold. If you spend a lot, the Lord of the Throne will never humiliate you.

O My servant. Obey Me and I will make you lordly, with ability to say to a thing 'Be!' and it will be.

Is there any mistake in that? If there is an error, the sin is on me. However, if you deny that *ḥadīth* and it is valid, the sin is on you!

Allāh Almighty orders our organs to speak and be true ones, and our hands, our legs, our tongues are going to speak truly! Therefore, that person will be astonishing, "How only my tongue was speaking? Now speaking my hands, my legs, my ears, my organs speaking also. How can it be?" They will say, *antaqan Allāhu allathi antaqa kulla shay'.*

May Allāh ﷻ forgive us.

Fātiḥah.

Questioning Erases Good Character

Aʿūdhu billāhi min ash-Shaytāni 'r-rajīm. Bismillāhi 'r-Raḥmāni 'r-Raḥīm. Dastūr, yā Sayyidī. Madad, yā rijālAllāh!

Allāhu Akbar, Allāhu Akbar, Allāhu Akbar, lā ilāha illa-Llāh. Allāhu Akbar, Allāhu Akbar wa lillāhi 'l-ḥamd, wa laka 'l-minna yā Rabbana ighfir lana mā madā yā wāsiʿya 'l-karami! For the honor of your most honored one from pre-Eternal to Eternal, Sayyidīna Muḥammad ﷺ, Sayyidi 'l-ʿAlamīn! Only He was granted to be Sayyidi 'l-Kawnayn, most high in Creation. No one can reach his level. He is the only one in the Divine Presence. Others, their heavenly levels are *akhireen*. Allāh Almighty's Will granted all praising and glorifying only to Sayyidīna Muḥammad ﷺ from pre-Eternal up to Eternal and Eternity. No one can understand that except the Lord of All Creation. He granted something to His most beloved one, Sayyidīna Muḥammad ﷺ. *Yā* Sayyidi, *yā Rasūlullāh*! We are also granting our most high salutes, our most high glorifying and praise that may be granted from creatures to you.

O our Master who is granted for looking after everything happening on this planet. O our Grandmaster, we are asking for your support and help. Your help is heavenly help and heavenly help is to stand up on our feet for our Lord's glorifying and praising!

As-salāmu ʿalaykum from east to west, those who are on this planet that was created by our Creator; those who are created by the will of the Lord of Creation!

O People! *As-salāmu ʿalaykum* once again, because every time we are saying to you *As-salāmu ʿalaykum,* it gives you honor. That is a heavenly salute for those who may accept it. Allāh Almighty is granting them much more lights and honor. Therefore, use it; say *As-salāmu ʿalaykum.* If you are not using it, you can't reach even one foot up from Earth. You will be on Earth; you will be under your feet. One day, your physical being is going to be taken under this Earth. Try for that time that the biggest grant from the Lord of Heavens to your holy being, your soul to be taken up to Heavens, to find its holy station, and to be happy forever.

O People! *As-salāmu ʿalaykum*! I am reaching to you a happiness and honor and lights forever, up to Eternal.

O People! Run after Eternity! Such a sweet word, Eternity! Eternity! *Azāliyūn, abādiyūn.* In all Creation, only one knows and understands what is pre-Eternal or Eternal. The Creator is not in need of understanding, but on behalf of the Lord of Heavens, only one is understanding Eternity. So refreshing for our souls that word, "Eternity," *Azāliyūn, abādiyūn, sarmadiyūn.*

O People! Don't ask something that you are not understanding. People yet are not reaching the level of understanding, such meanings as "Eternity."

O People! Try to learn. You can't learn by yourself if no one teaching. Even that one who is granted a sign from Eternity, is not understanding by himself: the Lord of Eternity must teach.

O People! Try to understand. Don't ask questions; questions are not for your level. Do you think that the Seal of Prophets ﷺ any time he asked anything from Archangel Gabriel? No. Because he is on the top line of *adab*, good manners. A good-mannered person is never asking anything. Because, what is our capacity? Only our Lord knows. He knows, but who is that one who is representing the Lord of Heavens? The representative is something and Who is granting to be His representative, that ocean no one can approach.

People are trying to ask so many questions. No good to ask questions. *al-ladhīqussima laka hāsil ladayk,* "What is granted to you from your Lord, your Creator, is just reaching to you." Why asking? For what you are asking? You learned everything and remaining only one to ask? Why not asking about servanthood? But people now are so proud, they think that they know or can understand everything.

Never! Never! No rights for a servant to ask something that is not for himself or for herself. They can't ask. If a person is invited to a sulṭān's presence, do you think that person asking something from the sulṭān? (Shaykh Hisham, 'No Sayyidī, *lā adab.*') The majesty of the sulṭān prevents him from asking anything, even one word more than he has been permitted. But people now have no *adab*! Asking, "This for what? That is for what?" What is your importance? Why you are asking? But you must learn everything first about yourself, then come to ask some questions.

There is no right for the Children of Adam to ask, except about servanthood. But they have no *adab* now, asking, "What is this, what is that?" That one represents Shaytān because the first one questioning was Shaytān, with no *adab*, asking his Creator, "Why You ordered for me to make *sajdah*?" That is *adab* for servanthood? He learned everything, but not understanding the Psalms, Old Testament, New Testament, and Holy Qur'an, mentioning, "Why He is ordering me to bow to Adam?" *Ptuu* (spit) on Shaytān, go away! But a mighty punch from the Lord of Heavens is striking that one and it sending away. "How can you ask Me why? Who is giving you that authority?"

Now all people have bad manners; they are saying, "Why He ordered this to us, why permitting this, not preventing that?" Who are you? Don't ask! Listen to the holy command from the Lord of Heavens, your Creator! Who is Shaytān to ask from his Creator, "Why are you ordering me to make *sajdah* to Adam?"

Who are you? That is good manners? From east to west, Christians, Jews, everyone now is asking! No one is coming to me and asking, "O servant of our Lord! What do you think about someone making a speech?" What is your answer?" It is so simple: my answer is, everything that people are asking is nonsense! Why you are not asking me about servanthood, or how does a person reach the Majestic Presence? He is asking, "O our king, why you are putting this there, why you are not putting down here?" That person is not saying, "Your Majesty," the protocol of people, and quickly he is removed from that presence! The first *adab* that Man must learn is good manners with his Creator!

Beyond this is not for him or for to ask. "Why Islam prevents women to show their faces?" Why you are asking me? Ask Who ordered you! I am not that One to answer you. Ask Who ordered women to protect themselves from Mankind. Ask Him ﷻ and take the answer. Do you think you can understand everything? Never! Don't speak and don't ask! We are only servants. What we have been ordered we must try to do and nothing else. If you come against heavenly orders you will be punished. You only can ask about servanthood, and from someone who is a servant.

The Seal of Prophets ﷺ is on the top point of servanthood, because the Lord of Heavens is saying, "I am only one Lord and that one, Sayyidīna Muḥammad ﷺ, is My representative." Allāh is saying, "You must ask him, not Me. I taught him servanthood and if you are not learning from him and coming to Me, I am sending you away, throwing you out." But people nowadays are getting proud, getting such instruments, looking at themselves, they are going to be such important ones. "I am important one and you are not important, you are nothing." A person can't be important in the Divine Presence until the Lord of Heavens is dressing that one in His servanthood. That one who is servant for their Lord and servant for Creation is going to be an important one. Others are nothing, of no value, garbage to be taken away.

If you are asking for honor in the Divine Presence, you must keep His servanthood. Servanthood can only be learned through a prophet that belongs to Heavens. They have been taught from Heavens to address people and then those people learn. If you are asking, "Why this, why that?" you are not on the level of servanthood and there are no rights for anyone to claim, "I am something." No German, no English, no Turkish, no Arab, no French. Germans will be angry, saying we must be 'those elite ones.' No, Allāh Almighty only created you and granted you an honor to be His deputies, His representatives. First of all, you must be a representative on yourself, not *ʿalā 'l-Ākhirīn*, on other people.

Because you have a heavenly being, your soul belongs to heavenly positions, and at the same time you have a physical being that belongs to earthly positions from Earth. The level of your physical being is on Earth and it is going to be in darkness. You must teach that one that belongs to darkness, "O my ego, the Lord of Heavens just enlightened you. Come out from darkness to enlightened levels of Heavens." That is first mission of the prophets, to call people, "Leave your ego and come out and join your heavenly being, to go up through enlightened worlds." If you are not accepting then you will be put in a bag and tied and thrown in one black hole and finished.

Therefore, they are going to ask on the Day of Resurrection, "O our Lord, now we are looking and understanding. Let us to go back to *dunyā* and to do our best for You." But divinely address coming, "If I am sending you back again a hundred times, you will run after darkness. Therefore, once is enough. You take the weight with you and go in black holes forever, finished. I am asking from My servants who are asking for light, lightening and enlightened worlds. I am granting to them because they were understanding, and using their understanding on that point. I am granting to them. You go away! You are having no chance to come back!"

O People! Try to understand something for your life! Don't be such a Shaytān, asking, 'Why, why, why?' If answer coming to Shaytān, 'Why he was ordered to bow to Adam,' then that illness is never ending, coming another 'why' and another 'why.' Therefore, *ṭarīqatu 'n-Naqshbandiyyāti 'l-*

ʿAliyyah, "the Most Distinguished Naqshbandi Sufi Order," is guiding people for their futures, here and Hereafter. Therefore, the most important, first condition that a Naqshbandi shaykh may teach and order to those people saying, "I like to be Naqshbandi" is this. If you truly want to be Naqshbandi, you must not ask, "Why!" and you must not say, "No!"

Any command comes to you, you must not say, "No, I am not doing it." So many things you may see throughout east and west but you cannot ask, "Why happening this, why happened that?" That is the most important thing in all religions, and in the most distinguished religion, Islam!

Islam is preparing people for their Lord's Divine Presence. Therefore, it is teaching, if coming to a sulṭān's presence, follow that protocol and don't ask anything; keep your tongue (silent)! If the sulṭān saying, then you must answer, "Yes, as you like, Sulṭān." And you know to say this to a man, so what then about your Lord, the Creator? Are you asking, "Why this, why that?" So now Mankind in the 21st Century are on point zero. They never understand for worshipping. They never understanding servanthood or what is real, good manners in the Divine Presence. Naqshbandi teaching is coming to teach people not to fight each other. It is coming to teach you to be best ones, so that you may be the best on the Day of Resurrection.

Allāh says be happy, therefore, I am making you to be happy! May Allāh ﷻ forgive us and guides us through His beloved ones, the most distinguished ones from His servants, to teach us to be as He likes.

Welcome to you from east to west! Shaykh Hisham Effendi is making me smile a little bit. If I am smiling, the whole world must smile!

Rabbī wa annahu huwa adhaka wa abka.

That it is He, Who grants laughter and tears. *53:43*

If not laughing, in this life they are never going to laugh.

May Allāh ﷻ forgive us.

Fātiḥah.

Stand Against Oppressors

A'ūdhu billāhi min ash-Shaytāni 'r-rajīm. Bişmillāhi 'r-Raḥmāni 'r-Raḥīm. Dastūr, yā Sayyidī. Madad, yā rijālAllāh!

Allāhu Akbar, Allāhu Akbar, Allāhu Akbar, lā ilāha illa-Llāh, Allāhu Akbar, Allāhu Akbar, wa lillāhi 'l-ḥamd! I am a Muslim. We are Muslims. No one can accuse me that I am not! *Ash-hadu 'alā ilāha illa-Llāh lā sharīka lah, wa ash-hadu anna Muḥammadan 'abduhu wa habībuhu wa Rasūluh, sallAllāhu 'alayhi wa sallam. Madad yā Sulṭān al-Awlīyā. Madad yā RijālAllāh. Madad yā Sāhib az-Zamān. Madad yā Sāhib al-Imdaad!*

As-salāmu 'alaykum, O human nature throughout east and west on this planet, on this *dunyā, as-salāmu 'alaykum!* I am asking Almighty Allāh's mercy on all of us. Please give your hearts for hearing. Don't be full with *shaytanic* bad attributes and dirty intentions. Shaytān always has bad intentions, never asking to be in his heart good intentions. Shaytān thrown away, thrown from the Heavenly Presence of the Lord of Heavens.

You, O Man! Always try to keep in your heart goodness, good luck, and good intentions for everyone. As much as you have such precious thinking in your heart, you will be closer to your Lord, Allāh Almighty.

I am a weak servant. According to a heavenly one's addressing, I am addressing you. Don't say that I know something or not. If I am knowing something, it is a grant from holy ones, and you must try to be holy ones: that is your good ending. If a person asking to be ended their lives in a good way, or better or best way, they must try to make their hearts full with mercy for all creatures. If you are carrying good intentions for every creature, they are giving to you what they have been granted from their Creator.

O People! O Mankind! Come and listen and think on it. *As-salāmu 'alaykum* once again, to carry you closer for a holy association or holy meeting, as you must follow the Seal of Prophets ﷺ, the teaching for all Creation what is best for them or for what they have been created, because no one can be able to be in front of their Creator and to speak, can't be! Can't be! He is Allāh Almighty, all-Merciful! No one knows about His Existence, *wujūd*; it is impossible for anyone to know the reality of His Existence, impossible!

O People! once again, *As-salāmu ʿalaykum*. This is a holy night in a holy month. Perhaps it is much more holy after Ramadan, Rajab, Shaʿbān; may be this month after them is most precious, most holy month through twelve months. And listen, because Allāh Almighty granted to Man for listening and for understanding, because the way of understanding is coming through ears as well as through your eyes. And we are all weak servants of our Lord, and we must be so humble, humble, humble!

O People! We must learn that the Seal of Prophets was saying, "*talaba 'l-ʿilmi farīdatun ʿalā kulli Muslim wa Muslimah.*" The holy Prophet ﷺ was saying to try for learning, it is an obligation on all believers, men and women. Therefore, we must learn or we must try to learn. From whom you must learn? Who knows, you must learn. Not from ignorant ones, no! Who knows, you may learn from that one. Don't be cheated by imitated titles. Imitated titles never giving an honor to Mankind, no! That is your grant, what you have that you are granted. If you have something, you are keeping for yourself, not giving to others. Yes. Imitated titles! People giving some of them for some others, no value. It is only for this limited life, *mu'akkat*, for temporary life, people enjoying to be said, "O graduated from where?" "That one is a doctor that graduated from....ha, ha, ha." They will be, our Salafi *ʿulama*, very angry. Doesn't matter. If they are angry, they are harming themselves, not harming me. What is the meaning of *Dār? "Ad-Dār Jala Jalāluhu,"* what does it mean? O *ʿulama*, you think you can harm someone, but you can't.

What does it mean, *ad-Dār*? You may be angry with me for some reason, but I am nothing! And you are saying, "We are something." You can't harm something that claims, "I am nothing!" What you are going to do for that one? Nothing! But who is saying they are something, holy order comes, "Cut their heads!" Because very serious shaykh this one (Shaykh Hisham). Speak to those serious shaykhs also, you Shaykh Hisham, never smiling! (Mawlana smiles.) Two heads cut, one cut down. For what? If a person saying nothing, how are you cutting nothing? *Astaghfirullāh, astaghfirullāh.*

When a person claims something without authority, divinely anger reaches that one and takes them away! We are saying we are now speaking from east to west, from up to down, downstairs, upstairs, we may speak. Some people are getting angry and maybe they think that they can do anything.

Hajjāj adh-Dhālim, a famous oppressor who was against Ahlu 'l-Bayt, peace be upon them, was in Baghdad and he heard about Sayyidīna Zayn al-'Abidīn. He asked, "Who is that one people are running after? I must speak to him, to understand who he is and try to make him know something about me. Bring him to me."

They brought Zayn al-'Abidīn ◈, who was then 14-years-old, and Hajjāj remained sitting, not giving t'adhīm, respect and honor to Prophet's ﷺ grandson.

He said, "Who are you?"

Zayn al-'Abidīn answered, "I am Zayn al-'Abidīn. Who are you?"

Little by little, Hajjāj adh-Dhālim became angry, saying, "O young one! Are you not fearing from my position and haybat, power? You are not fearing from me? I can order the executor to cut your head. Are you not fearing?"

With so much conviction and confidence and faith, Zayn al-'Abidīn ◈ answered, "O Hajjāj! There is yet no news that the Lord of Heavens gives authority for you to order Angel Azra'il to take my soul! Don't say such things, as we are from the Seal of Prophets ﷺ, Habībullāh's descendants! You can't say this to me! I do not fear your shouting! What you are saying is for you and not for me!"

Baytu 'l-hikmah wa baytu 'l-'ilm, Sayyidīna 'Ali, karamAllāhu wajahah, Family of wisdom and family of knowledge, the descendants of Sayyidīna 'Ali, may Allāh ennoble his face.

Hajjāj adh-Dhālim was trembling before that boy and ordered his guards to quickly release him to go as he likes.

This is a suitable story for those who are thinking, "We can kill, cut, and injure people." No. You can't harm, kill, or do anything Allāh Almighty does not ask to be done for that person. If the Lord of Heavens protects a person, no one will do anything.

Once in the month Safar, the Prophet ﷺ was in battle and he ﷺ and the Saḥābah stopped on a plateau. Saḥābah took their rest and Rasūlullāh ﷺ went a slight distance away from them to a tree where he rested. Suddenly, one Bedouin appeared and drew his sword, saying, "O Muḥammad! Now who can save you from my sword?"

Prophet ﷺ answered, "Allāh!"

Immediately that Arab fell down and the sword fell out of his hands.

Rasūlullāh ﷺ took his the sword, saying, "Now, who can save you from this sword!?"

People think Islam is based on fairytales. *Ptuu* (spit) on them; they will be under Earth. This is *dīnullāh,* Allāh Almighty's religion that He is ordering to His servants, "Come to Islam!" When the Seal of Prophets ﷺ sent his holy letter to the viceroy of Rome, Caesar of Constantinople, it was written first, "Come to Islam and be in safety, here and Hereafter." Therefore, so many people may be angry with what we are saying.

If you say, "We can harm a person, or do our best for anyone," you are on the wrong way. You must believe that Allāh Almighty granting or taking His grant.

O People! *As-salāmu ʿalaykum.* Don't be heedless. I am not asking from *dunyā* but so many people with imitated titles asking for *dunyā* because it is under my feet. I am on my way to my Lord and you are thinking you are never going to be in Holy Presence of your Lord. You are making trouble The commander of this planet is making my tongue to speak about real Islam and its reality! If not, you may fear that by morning you may dies in your bed! Beware! Prophet ﷺ said:

> *It may be that a curly-haired, dusty person asks Allāh for anything; Allāh will respond to him immediately.*
> Muslim

Someone with unkempt hair, dusty, if he were to swear an oath by Allāh, Allāh would fulfill it. Don't look at a person's dressing. There are so many people that can't find anything for dressing as you like, but their words go up to the Lord of Heavens, Who may say, "My servant is asking, and I must grant it." It is a long story for awakening. I am not asking to be a *malik* (king), to be a grand shaykh, to be a viceroy, no. All of them are useless. All titles that people give to you have no reality. Don't be cheated, but try to take a title from the Divinely Presence. That is our last desire, for which the Lord of Heavens is calling, "O My servant! *Yā ʿabdī, yā ʿabdī, yā ʿabdī*!

Don't claim that you know everything, no. Don't say your opinions are true and others are wrong, no. Keep your *adab* with Sāhib al-Adab, Rasūlullāh ﷺ, and Allāh will protect you and accept you.

First of all, I am asking for forgiveness, but they are making a weak and old servant to address all people from east to west. If anyone is saying that is wrong or not true, the responsibility is on me, not on them. They may say what is true and what is wrong with what they are saying.

May Allāh forgive me, and forgive them, and forgive you for the honor of Sayyidīna Muḥammad ﷺ!

O People! You must know that if anyone is trying to be like someone else, he and that one are on the same way. You must know who you are following! Are they on *haqq* or *bātil*? That is an important warning. Beware.

May Allāh ﷻ forgive us.

Fātiḥah.

Only One Is in the Divine Presence

A'ūdhu billāhi min ash-Shaytāni 'r-rajīm. Biṣmillāhi 'r-Raḥmāni 'r-Raḥīm. Dastūr, yā Sayyidī. Madad, yā rijālAllāh!

Allāhu Akbar, Allāhu Akbar, Allāhu Akbar, lā ilāha illa 'Llah wa-Llahu Akbar, Allāhu Akbar wa lillāhi 'l-ḥamd! You only are the Creator, the Lord from pre-Eternal up to Eternal. No one is with you. No God except You, our Creator, Lord of All Creation. No son for You, no partner for You. Everything, they are your creatures. O People! He is only One, our Lord! *Allāh Allāh, Allāh Allāh, Allāh Allāh, Allāh Allāh.* You are Only One, and representing you is only one real deputy. No one knows when that one was in existence, but *'Lā ilāha illa-Llāh'* was not alone and behind it was *'Muḥammadan 'abduhu wa habībuhu wa Rasūluh.'*

That is real belief that may save you here and Hereafter. We are asking all praising and all glory granted from Allāh to that one, Sayyidīna Muḥammad ﷺ. Stand up for his honor!

O People! We are all imitated deputies, and only one crown prince for one king. Who is that? Even if a king has a hundred children, there is only one crown prince; they are deputies but actually, one.

O People! Try to learn. To learn is a heavenly order to all Mankind. Everything is knowing; everything in existence are not dead ones. If dead ones, never saying Allāh Almighty":

wa in min shay'in illa yusabbihu bī ḥamdih.

There is not a thing but celebrates His praise. *17:44*

Everything is glorifying their Creator, Allāh Almighty, and their glorifying can't reach to the Divinely Presence; may be prophets, *awlīyā* or angels. No one's glorifying can reach to the Divinely Presence. That is important. That means everything that is in existence are living ones. If they are not living ones, how they are glorifying? Can't be.

An atom is alive, a living one, but their lives different to the lives of some others. And no one knows the number of Creation; no one knows their living and glorifying from every planet or every level of Heavens. No one knows about those ones that are alive. And don't think that they are all glorifying their Lord in the same way. *SubḥānAllāh*! Each atom's glorifying is different from the second one and no one knows the number of atoms, electrons or neutrons. *SubḥānAllāh*! Those people who are researching about atoms, their eyes are closed, their eyes are not open. No opening! They have so much knowledge, perhaps hundreds of books about atoms, and they are never witnessing but they only may put theories, this and that. But no one is knowing the real being of an atom or electron, and they are saying the nucleus of an atom is perhaps forty different pieces. And each one has a private creation; private station, private condition for every one.

People who are reading about atoms are saying electrons have a negative power and nucleus has another kind of being. What they are looking and not seeing, they can witness and say that in a nucleus of an atom perhaps may be more or less ten different pieces. Each piece representing only itself; and one hydrogen atom is not same as a second hydrogen atom. Each one has a special being, special existence, special identity.

They are so astonished, because it is only positive and negative, but when they are coming deeply their minds showing them something else that is beyond their understanding, it can't be so different?

What about for Mankind? Allāh Almighty is Creator, and each one's glorifying (He made) is different. Billions, trillions, I am not saying billions, trillions of atoms; I am speaking now about billions and trillions of oceans, Power Oceans! Those oceans are under the hegemony of the Creator; He is creating that!

O People! We don't know anything. Now time is over. This planet is going to end and our Creator just sent us so many prophets. You can't say on behalf of a real deputy, no. Allāh is sending and His Absolute Deputy is only one, AHMAD ﷺ! Therefore, his name just mentioned in Old Testament, New Testament, Psalms and all heavenly books, and also the last heavenly book that reached to people on this planet, *ʿadhīmu-shān*, Holy Qur'an. That is just coming in the way of that one, the Absolute Deputy for Creation, Sayyidīna Muḥammad ﷺ. And no one is knowing what the Seal of Prophets ﷺ is knowing; he is an ocean of Oceans! All oceans are taking their material from that one's ocean; and each ocean, no one can be able to reach its beginning or ending!

Therefore, Allāh Almighty sending Jesus Christ, 'Isa ﷺ as a miracle, *muʿjizah*, without a father. People always using *their* balance. Who are you, and what is your balance going to scale? But people asking to bring heavenly understanding. They are not trying to reach Heavens, but they are asking to bring from Heavens some realities in front of them. They are foolish people. Do you think that for understanding Venus, for example, it is like a spot in space. What do you think if a person is saying, "I must bring that one and to look." May you take that one in front of you to look at it, or are you going there? But people are so foolish, asking everything from spirituality to bring understanding to their material beings.

In his assembly, Prophet ﷺ was always making people to be in Hālatu 'l-Bast, the State of Joy. Therefore, this no-mind one coming beside me and taking, *Māshā'Allāh*. Allāh Almighty likes to make people happy but Salafi *'ulama* are very serious ones. What is your seriousness? You must be happy that you have been created, coming in existence, be happy! No-mind people. Ahmed also very important, all of us important ones. *Huuu*.

That is their position in our times. People are not understanding from spirituality. They are always asking a proof from their material beings. It can't be. How can you bring Mars here, to look at it? What is that foolishness? You may reach there and you may look and understand; not for Mars to come to you and you look what is in it. Like no-mind Chechnya one, "I am a very serious person." (Laughter) If people don't like to be enjoyful, what I can do? I am sending them to the WC (bathroom) center, to be very serious there.

And Christians it is a *yaqīn 'ilm*, knowledge of certainty, they are leaving that and trying to make something that even ants can laugh to them. Today people thinking that it is a holy day for Christians. That is their saying Christmas day. Never written in holy books. What they are doing this and saying, "You are doing theater. Making your religion theater." Every year, every year repeating. What you are understanding? Every year you are bringing St. George, who is that one, St. Nicholas, Pai Nikola. I am sorry to say that even Muslims now are becoming so ignorant ones, because they are running after westernizing.

They are saying, "We must try to be like Western people." I am asking, what is Western peoples' honor, or ranks over "westernized" people, because you are not believing such things and making us down and making their theaters up. Jesus Christ did such a thing? No. But it is such a big blame for Muslims. I am looking everywhere, Muslims trying to be like Christians. They are trying to be like Christians and congratulating each other, "Happy New Year." What is "Happy New Year"? What is this, where is it written New Year; this is New Year?

The gospels of Barnabas, Luke, John, Matthew, and Mark are saying to do this? And finally, I am asking them, do you think you have four gospels? Do you think that just four gospels coming from Heavens? Why you are not bringing to me Jesus Christ's gospel? I am asking for that one. I am not asking for Luke, John, Matthew, or Mark. I am not asking for those gospels, but the gospel coming from Heavens to Jesus Christ, where is it?

I am surprised that Muslim *ʿulama*, particularly the Salafi *ʿulama*, are not making a *fatwa* (judicial ruling) that those who celebrate Christmas night and New Year's night are *kāfir*!

man tashabbah bi-qawmin fa huwa minhum.

Who imitates a people is from them. ~*Muslim*

Why they are not making a *fatwa?* They are saying, "Shaykh is speaking from downstairs to upstairs." What I know, I am saying to you. I am defending Holy Qur'an and holy books, but my speech style is different. I know their knowledge, but they don't know what I know! I know their powers, but they don't know my powers because they are saying, "We are something," and I am saying, "I am nothing!" To be nothing is much more powerful than to be something!

The Last Days are approaching and this declaration is appearing in the Holy Qur'an, and they are making me to come down to the first level for speaking. I know how to speak on higher, higher, higher levels, but it is not for me. I have been ordered to address people, to make them sometimes happy and sometimes thinking. I am not collecting money; they are collecting money and I am saying, "Take it with you to the cemetery."

O People! *As-salāmu ʿalaykum*! Use your mind for understanding, for reaching Allāh Almighty's pleasure. If you are trying to make your Lord pleased with you, you will be pleased ones. If you are asking to give pleasure to your Creator, Allāh Almighty, your life is going to be in pleasure. If you are trying to make the Lord of Heavens happy with you, then you will be happy here and Hereafter.

May Allāh ﷻ forgive us.

Aslih shānuna wa shān al-muslimīn wa adhir sharaf habībika, Sayyidi 'l-Awwalīn wa 'l-Ākhirīn.

When heavenly lightening comes on this planet, there will be no more crisis. Leave the "economical crisis;" throw it in the WC!

May Allāh forgive us, and forgive me and blessing you, for the honor of His most honored one, blessing me and you. They can make me speak up to next Jumu'ah or next month or next year, or up to end of this year, and it will never finish. I do not know, but when I am sitting here they are making me to speak. I am nothing.

May Allāh ﷻ forgive us.

Fātiḥah.

Use the Heavenly Sword of Protection

A'ūdhu billāhi min ash-Shaytāni 'r-rajīm. Bismillāhi 'r-Raḥmāni 'r-Raḥīm. Dastūr, yā Sayyidī. Madad, yā rijālAllāh!

Allāhu Akbar, Allāhu Akbar, lā ilāha illa-Llāh, Allāhu Akbar, Allāhu Akbar, wa lillāhi 'l-ḥamd! Iqtubna ma' ash-shahidīn yā Mawlay. Nahnu mu'minīn, muslimīn w 'alā dhālika maqbūlīn. Yā Rabbi fī mithl hādhihi al-laylah bī jāh Nabiyyaka 'l-Karīm, sannid umūrana amiddana bī madadin khās bī jāhi Nabiyyika al-karīm. Thumma alfu salāt, alfu salām for Your most glorified servant, Sayyidīna Muḥammad ﷺ. *Dastūr yā Sayyidī, yā Sulṭān al-Awlīyā.*

As-salāmu 'alaykum, O Mankind, all of you! Be thankful that you have been chosen from the countless creatures to be from Children of Adam ﷺ, as Allāh Almighty created Adam ﷺ to be His deputy. You must be happy, you must be thankful, you must be enjoyful! *As-salāmu 'alaykum* once again. If you like to reach high stations of Heavens, give respect to your Lord, Who created everything, and you must be thankful to Allāh Almighty from pre-Eternal up to Eternal. Say, *a'ūdhu billāhi min ash-Shaytāni 'r-rajīm.* Run away, try to run away from Shaytān! Those who are running away from Shaytān are running to their Lord, to their Creator.

O People! You must know who is your most terrible enemy, most jealous or envious one, Shaytān. He is never happy with what you have been granted. Ask for heavenly protection. Don't say, "We are running to Allāh." *Allāhu Akbaru 'l-Akbar!* As a servant, if someone is attacking him, he will not run to the sulṭān and say, "Save me, O Sulṭān!" But he must run to someone who is authorized to save him, who has enough authority and enough power to keep Shaytān away from him, enough, taking you in and throwing your enemy out.

When you are coming to the guardian of your Lord's Throne, that guardian or guard is enough to make your enemy to run away, not to come back. Therefore, Mankind must learn everything that gives them benefit here and Hereafter. And for our protection physically and spiritually, you must run to your Lord. And every guard they are also representing all creatures for guarding them and for sending away their enemy. Weakest one, it is enough. Angels are representing Allāh Almighty's creatures who are always coming out from the oceans of Creation. *Huuuu.* One of them is enough, but you must run to that one!

Therefore, we are saying, *a'ūdhu billāhi min ash-Shaytāni 'r-rajīm,* because the Lord of Heavens is ordering that you may ask protection from your worst enemy, wildest one who has no mercy in his heart for you! You may run to your Lord's protection and sheltering. Those who run to shelter under heavenly sheltering, he will be sheltered. That is a very important point to know for everyone. Don't say, "I am powerful enough to keep Shaytān away." Impossible, impossible! You must run to your Lord's sheltering. Allāh Almighty's sheltering, nothing can break it and come on you, no.

And we are saying, also when we are running for a sheltering we must say, *Bismillāhi 'r-Raḥmāni 'r-Raḥīm.* O my Lord's servant! Take this heavenly sword and try to defend yourself. You are now in this life, on this planet. Don't think that when you are asking for sheltering, Allāh Almighty is sending to you armies of angels, but He is granting you a sword. What is that sword? *Bismillāhi 'r-Raḥmāni 'r-Raḥīm.* Use it! Shaytān, if it is not only one, or one million, billion, trillion, quadrillion, if you are surrounded by the number of atoms of shaytans, they can't touch you. If it touches you, it will be thrown away.

I was a small one, people thinking I am always a young one, like me now. (laughter) At 'Eid time there was a big place where everyone came with their children, selling, showing, to make small ones happy with 'Eid celebrations. Once I was going with my elder brothers and saw one man sitting there, his fez covered his forehead and his eyes were closed. On his table there was a cup of water, and he said, "O children! Come give one penny and take one shilling. Give one shilling, take five shillings. Put five shillings, take ten shillings. Put ten shillings, take one pound! Pay half-penny, look in a pot." It was the time of late Queen Victoria, but it was silver.

I will do here for you, put your hand and take. And children coming, some new one coming, paying half-penny and saying, "Now when I am saying to you, put your hand in it and take," and he was making something here, *ring, ring, ring,* "Now take!" Making like this and that (hand in and out of the pot and shaking their body). And he was saying, "If you are not taking, half-penny for me and your half-shilling there. I take just one penny for me, for you here, take it. I am not preventing you." And children coming and trying again, *ring, ring, ring.* Small ones not understanding. They were putting their hand and shaking their bodies for three times in a row, because that person placed electricity in water and if anyone put their hand in the water they got an electrical shock.

Now people may say, "We may defend ourselves before Shaytān by ourselves, it is not necessary to say, *aʿūdhu billāhi min ash-Shaytāni 'r-rajīm*, or to say, *Bismillāhi 'r-Raḥmāni 'r-Raḥīm*." They are so ignorant ones! Now, 99 percent of people are not believing in spirituality. Everything in their eyes is only for a material world and material life. And they are seeing he is representing a spiritual being on Earth, but they are making themselves as a rock or a tree. They are saying, "We have enough mind and cleverness for defending ourselves. Why should we say, *Bismillāhi 'r-Raḥmāni 'r-Raḥīm*?" Then they don't say it and they are falling down!

This is a very important point which is granted to Mankind, a very special power granted in (reciting), *Bismillāhi 'r-Raḥmāni 'r-Raḥīm*. Three names of Allāh Almighty is giving that protection. If anyone is saying, *Bismillāhi 'r-Raḥmāni 'r-Raḥīm*, he has been granted an Unseen power for defending himself. Therefore, now perhaps 99 percent of people are not believing in spirituality and always they are falling down. Their works and efforts are always going to be on zero point. They can't be able to improve, because they are saying, "Our minds or our mentalities or our knowledge is enough to defend us." If you are saying this, save yourself!

What happened? They are saying, "U.S. is falling in a very bad situation by the economical crisis." Why, because you have such a power! You are saying you have enough knowledge to defend yourselves, so how did this happened?! Where did trillions dollars disappear to?! You said before, "We can defend ourselves before any crisis," so yes, do it now. They are saying, "We are bankrupt, finished." How can it be? That is the meaning! If a person not controlling their powers, they can't be able to do anything. Now, yes, you have enough cleverness, you have economical doctors, you are this or that.

What you are doing? Just one year now, whole world coming down and I am saying why are you not using your mind? If you are saying, "We can use our physical being to save ourselves," then why you are crying and kicking yourself like horses? For what? What changed? Nothing changed. If you look, nothing changed. But you are saying that there is an economical crisis. Where is it? How was it done? Why? What is the real reason? The Lord of Heavens is closing that tap and now you are saying, "Before our water was running, what happened now?"

Yes, I was a small one also and water under roads were running through pipes. Sometimes there is an obstruction in the pipe and then water is not coming and there were some special people to understand the reason, seeing some pipe were harmed and there is a hole, water coming out, not going there.

O People! Don't say that you know everything, no! If you know everything, quickly you can find what is the reason the economical crisis appeared. What is the reason? I know, and I may say to them, but first I must ask our Salafi *'ulama,* what is your opinion? "We are never looking at such things, we are looking at *āyatul karīmah* or *ḥadīthu Nabawī ash-sharīfah,* and only understanding Qur'an and *ḥadīth.*" I am saying, Qur'an *sharīf* or *ḥadīth sharīf* you are not understanding, because you are not looking to find *hikmah,* wisdom!

I am asking, how will people be saved from the economical crisis? If you don't know, don't say that you are *'ulama.* I am nothing, but something is coming to my heart and I may speak to you! Sayyidīna Muḥammad ﷺ was granted the Holy Qur'an, last heavenly message up to the Day of Judgment. How come you are not finding a way to save people from the economical crisis? Why are you not making a declaration, "O People! we have an exit."

O Salafi *'ulama*! Where are you? Why are you not showing people what is right and what is wrong? Allāh Almighty will ask you on the Day of Resurrection, "Why you are not teaching My holy book's verses for people to understand? Why you are not saying this to believers, Muslims and *mu'mins*?" Do you think, Salafi *'ulama* that Ummati Muḥammad ﷺ are on the right way now? If you are saying yes, you are liars! Ummat Sayyidīna Muḥammad ﷺ!

All of them are on the wrong way. For what? What is their measure, what are their ways? Do you think they are on Sirātul Mustaqīm (the Straight Path), or on *ghayril mustaqīm* (crooked)? What do they worry about their people and themselves; what are they thinking? What is their *dīni,* belief? Do you think kings of the *ummah* only worry how they will be a westernized state? All kings and presidents under every kind of sulṭān are only thinking for their names not to be written on the list of states not following westernized civilization, because western people are looking if they are following or not. And they are trying to show that they are following westernized countries step-by-step, so that their degrees are not degraded (in western view).

O Salafi *'ulama*! are you saying this to people or not? Leaders of organization of Islamic countries are running after westernizing! Why are you not saying that is *kufr*? Allāh ﷻ and Prophet ﷺ are never accepting. Don't swear at me, swear at yourself!

They don't like what I am saying. What is coming to my heart, I am speaking. Say this is wrong! They can't say. Anyone who is not accepting truth, cursing is coming on their heads! What can save Muslim countries from falling into economical crisis? Tell me! Send one *fatwa* to me! And if main solution and saving Islamic world from economical crisis, one *ḥadīth* I am speaking to you to whole world from east to west, north to south. You may write this with golden letters, what Sayyidīna Muḥammad ﷺ was saying, *Bismillāhi 'r-Raḥmāni 'r-Raḥīm.*

O Salafi *'ulama*! The greatest cursing coming on the *ummah*, what is the reason? How are the kings and shaykhs of petrol stations living, say to me! Are they keeping that *ḥadīth*? Allāh Almighty is warning them! How? Say! Shaytān is making people fall in a deepless hole. This *israf* it is like a black hole and anyone who falls in it never gets out because the nation of the last Prophet, Sayyidīna Muḥammad ﷺ, is not following his way. They are not following what he is directing them for saving themselves here and Hereafter. They are on the wrong way, and asking to exit the economical crisis. You are not going on that way, you are going in the opposite way, and they are falling into black holes. Everyone is now in a black hole, (making a sound) *wooooooh, woooooh.* No way, finished.

The nation of the Seal of Prophets ﷺ lost the way which guides them to Paradise, here and Hereafter. That is the reason. Don't swear at me, because sometimes my *munajāt* (supplication) may reach you, or one of your member's family or people. Then you may cry, so don't swear at me. I am sometimes a very easy one, a very weak one, and sometimes a very strong one. When I am saying through the tongue of the Seal of Prophets, Sayyidīna Muḥammad ﷺ, no one can blame me; blame yourself.

It is a holy night and this bombarding is for Shaytān's batteries! I am also bombarding people who are supporters of Shaytān. Even one cigarette supports Shaytān and is destroying *Shari`atullāh.* One *argeela,* for what? Why you are not speaking about it? Do you only know how to call people *mushrik* and *kāfir,* is that your knowledge? Are you not ashamed? Do you not fear Allāh ﷻ, to call *kāfir* someone who says, *Ash-hadu an lā ilāha illa-Llah, wa ash-hadu anna Muḥammadan Rasūluh*?

But time is over now, the time of revenge for every wrong one. If I am wrong, He knows to take me away also. Everyone that is coming and closing the way of *huda* (guidance), they will fall down. I don't know in this month, this year, or after this year, such heavy approaching.

O People! May Allāh ﷻ forgive me and grant His blessings to be on us and we are asking to be sent to whole *ummah* one powerful one for saving them from falling into a black hole. A big black hole is now swallowing the *ummah*, also.

Tawbah yā Rabbī, tawbah yā Rabbī, tawbah yā Rabbī, tawbah astāgfirullāh!

Allāh Allāh, Allāh Allāh, Allāh Allāh, ʿAzīz Allāh
Allāh Allāh, Allah Allāh, Allāh Allāh, Karīm Allāh
Allāh Allāh, Allah Allāh, Allāh Allāh, Subḥān Allāh
Allāh Allāh, Allāh Allāh, Allāh Allāh, Sulṭān Allāh

Amīn, yā Rabbī. They (Salafi *ʿulama*) are hiding real commands of the Heavens. They are not advising the *ummah* and they are showing right way to be westernized, not to be like before. We shall see. I am asking for forgiveness. *Astaghfirullāh, astaghfirullāh, astaghfirullāh, astaghfirullāh, tawbah, astaghfirullāh.*

May Allāh ﷻ forgive us.

Fātiḥah.

Everything Is Held by Allah Almighty

Aʿūdhu billāhi min ash-Shaytāni 'r-rajīm. Bişmillāhi 'r-Raḥmāni 'r-Raḥīm. Dastūr, yā Sayyidī. Madad, yā rijālAllāh!

Lā ilāha illa-Llāh, lā ilāha illa-Llāh, lā ilāha illa-Llāh Sayyidīna wa Nabiyyina, Mawlana Muḥammad Rasūlullāh ﷺ zidhu yā Rabbī ʿizzan wa sharafan nūran wa masrūran ridwānan wa ṣulṭānan faktub hādha shahādat ʿindaka yā Rabbana nahnu mu'minīn muslimīn muʿtiyyīn ʿabidīn ijaʿalna zahidīn yā Rabbi 'l-ʿAlamīn.

As-salāmu ʿalaykum, our listeners who are giving a short time for their Eternal lives. You are given a short life and a short time, but from your 24 hours you are never taking care to give even a few moments, and you are claiming you are graduated, clever ones. Try to take your heavenly graduation; not to take graduation from this imitated life. They are asking from our grandmaster, who is responsible for everything that is happening on this planet. People may say, how can he be responsible for everything on this planet, it is so big? It is not a difficult matter to give an authority to one atom to guide this whole world. Allāh Almighty is saying so many times, perhaps 70 times in the Holy Qur'an, *laʿllahum yatafakkarūn, laʿllakum tatafakkarūn,* "In order that they/you may consider."

If you are trying to think, that thinking is the way to real knowledge. If a person is not thinking, he can't find a way to true understanding. Enough! It is enough for Allāh Almighty to grant very, very, very, very small; smaller than an atom to say to others. Allāh Almighty addressing to everything. But what He is addressing to a Man is something else and to address any other creation is something else. To command an atom is something else, also. And His holy command is reaching everything. If He is bringing a creature into life in existence, He must say, "Come out! Be an atom."

> *Innamā amruhu idhā arāda shayan an yaqūla lahu kun fa yakūn.*
>
> *Verily, when He intends a thing His command is, 'Be' and it is!* 36:82

"You be a planet, you be a galaxy, you be instantly a black hole. You 'be' instantly; before My order finishes you must be in existence." He is Allāh Almighty!

Man's honor is with his knowledge and an ignorant one, no value. And the honor of Man is with his knowledge and understanding. You are granted an honor according to your understanding, but when you are making it less, less, less, and then you will be behind one. Now we are zero behind one, on right hand. Same zero going to take an honor when that zero is standing on the right side of one. When you are putting it in front of one, it is going to lose everything, no value.

Now they are trying to be someone or something, but they are not thinking that to be something also is either *yakūn* on right hand or *yakūn* on left hand. Something is granted from the Lord of Heavens, our Creator, on the right hand, given 10, 100, 1000, 10,000, 100,000 millions, billions, trillions, quadrillions. Going on, because that is grant from the Lord of Creatures. Who is asking to be something and is trying to give his highest glorifying, the Lord of Heavens is giving to that one something, something, something.

That 'something' never belongs to the endless dominions of Allāh Almighty. No, that is an appearance, as you are looking in a mirror, you are looking and finding yourself in it, but that is not a real one. No, real one is here, but what you are seeing in a mirror is something you can see only, you can't touch. That existence of yourself in the mirror is nothing, but your Lord is asking to give to you (an existence) not like that, what you ask to be 'something.' You are just granted something that you may look (see) in a mirror and out of the mirror you can't be anything. May Allāh ﷻ forgive us.

O People! *As-salāmu ʿalaykum.* I am a weak servant but what they are giving to me is for understanding, because understanding is not material and if not material, it is going, going, going; no way or no beginning that you may run after it. But that beginning and ending is not like your Lord's, *qidām wa baqā,* continuous existence from pre-Eternal to Eternal. Therefore, no one is knowing what is pre-Eternal or Eternal.

O People! All of us must try to understand something that is suitable for our mentality and the largeness of our understanding. Therefore, we are saying, *As-salāmu ʿalaykum,* O our Lord's creatures! From one to one there is some connection; no one can be alone. Every atom is going to be in relation or in connection to what its right hand or left hand or front or back or up or down must know. And must know with which style of glorifying of Allāh, this one, this one, this one, or up and down? There must be harmony in everything. Our minds can't be able to understand that harmony between two atoms, four atoms, and six atoms.

Hasānati Qudrah, Greatness of the Creator that is only granted for Creation. It is not the glory of *dhāt,* essence, no. And harmony for an atom must be such a fine arrangement. One atom is just surrounded from six directions. That creation can't be there if one of those is lost or disappears, then finishing.

innallāha yumsiku 's-samāwāti wa 'l-arda an tazūla.

It is Allāh Who sustains the Heavens and the Earth unless they cease (to function). *35:41*

That is Arabic. I am asking to doctors and Salafi *ʿulama* or Christian learned people, what is your understanding for that holy verse? Give a meaning. How the Lord of Heavens is just holding? How? That one only, the Lord of Heavens, the Creator of Earth and Heavens, how is He keeping them? Everything in it, even an atom, or less than an atom, must be held by the Creator's Mighty Hands. If His Mighty Hands not keeping, just running away from existence to non-existence, finished. Therefore, everything, an atom or less than an atom, must be kept in six directions. It must be protected and kept in existence by the mighty power of the Creator.

O *ʿulama*! Hear and try to understand. If Allāh Almighty is not keeping every creature in existence, nothing is going to be in existence. His heavenly Power Oceans must catch everything in existence, from six directions, to be in existence or seen in existence. Therefore, the meaning of *lā ilāha illa-Llāh*; those people asking to run into Unknown Oceans of divine knowledge are saying that if Allāh Almighty is not keeping everything in its situation, just going to melt, or become 'unseen,' or reach endless Power Oceans and finished. When Allāh ﷻ is asking something to come in appearance, saying, "Come," and everything is appearing!

O People! *As-salāmu ʿ alaykum.* We are asking *salāmat.* Safety or good understanding about yourself, everything around yourself and everything around this planet.

Wamā qadarullāha haqqa qadrih.

No just estimate have they made of Allāh, what is due to Him. *39:67*

No one knows. Therefore, Allāh Almighty is ordering His Last, most-honored Messenger to ask from Him only:

Wa qul Rabbī zidni ʿilma.

And say, "O my Lord, increase me in knowledge." 20:114

Where are our Muslims' ways, where they are going, what Allāh Almighty is saying to His most glorified servant, "O My most glorified servant, don't ask from Me anything except to give to you more knowledge." That knowledge is only for Creation. From Creation you may reach a level of knowing Allāh Almighty's existence!

There are so many knowledges now. Don't ask, this for what or that for what. Every branch of heavenly knowledge must take you to the existence of the Lord of Heavens. You are teaching your students and every knowledge is taking you to know the Absolute Existence of the Lord of Creation. Are you teaching? No, you are just teaching, *rawā* Anas ibnu Mālik ؓ, *rawā* Muadh ibn Jabal ؓ, *rawā* Abū Hurayrah ؓ, but what is in it? You know?

For that knowledge they are speaking and asking to teach something. I am not *hāfiz* of all *hadīth as-sharīf*. I know ten or perhaps twenty declarations of Rasūlullāh ﷺ, but everything that I am knowing from the Seal of Prophets ﷺ is such an endless ocean. And endless oceans of learning or knowledge are taking you to your Lord's Divine Existence, *muwajjahah*. Taking you from you to Him. "Taking you," means you will be nothing. Then, when you are nothing, just appearing the signs of existence of your Lord, Allāh Almighty.

If your knowledge is not taking you to a level, then you can't be able to understand anything from your Creator. That is also a deepless ocean. Therefore, every atom or less than atom is leading you to the existence of the Creator of Creation, of creatures. You can't say, "I learned this or I learned that." But you must follow that way that is taking servants to their Lord's Divine Presence. *Allāh, Allāh.*

O People! We are saying, *a'ūdhu billāhi min ash-Shaytāni 'r-rajīm. Bismillāhi 'r-Rahmāni 'r-Rahīm.* O our Lord, protect us from Shaytān and his assistants, because they are making for our understanding to be upset or never leaving for anyone a good or perfect understanding. First for all, to know Allāh ﷻ is *ma'rifatullāh*. You have been ordered to know about your Creator. Perhaps we are going to a level and saying, "It is enough for me." Behind every horizon is appearing another one. Therefore, endless levels of *ma'rifatullāh*, to know our Lord's Divinely Being, perhaps up to Eternal never going to end.

Therefore, it is so strange that you are seeing and learning something else that never passed before, or never coming to you that answer. Every time, every moment, *waridāt,* inspirations every moment, never-ending heavenly inspirations; always you can find from heavenly inspirations and that is giving us a pleasure. Every time inspirations are opening and that person is looking and finding such a beauty and refreshment; a sweetness is coming that you never ask to leave and go back, but are always running after that inspiration to find much more happiness and refreshment and sweetness in yourself and to feel an honor that you can't be able to think on it.

Therefore, all prophets were ordering people, "O People! Try to be more understanding ones from heavenly positions and there will be more pleasure for you, forever. You are not going to be fed up. In every moment and every second you can find a new view and inspirations and knowledge that never passed before."

O People! We must try to find more and more. Therefore, we have been ordered to follow Sāhibu 'l-'Ilm ﷺ, who knows about this life or next life. It gives everything to you; a new taste, a sweetness, a new glorifying and new mighty powers that belong to creatures. Not saying power for Allāh ﷻ, Allāh has no need, but that power in you is going to be only for you and for everyone on that same level.

That is why Allāh Almighty ordering to his most beloved servant, Sayyidīna Muḥammad ﷺ! *Yā Rabb, wa qul rabbi zidnī 'ilma. Zidnī yā Rabb, zidna yā Rabb.* That knowledge cleans our physical beings, cleans our mentalities, cleans our knowledge, giving us lights. Lightening appearing in your real beings, enlightened like sun, like moon and like stars. Try to reach like heavenly moons, suns and stars; that gives to you enjoyment here and Hereafter. May Allāh ﷻ forgive us.

Allāh Allāh, Allāh Allāh, Allāh Allāh, 'Azīz Allāh
Allāh Allāh, Allāh Allāh, Allāh Allāh, Karīm Allāh
Allāh Allāh, Allāh Allāh, Allāh Allāh, Subhān Allāh
Allāh Allāh, Allāh Allāh, Allāh Allāh, Sulṭān Allāh

May Allāh forgive us for the honor of the most honored one in His Divinely Presence, Sayyidīna Muḥammad ﷺ.

O People! Before going to be repented, try at least to hear such speeches and hear something from such extraordinary Knowledge Oceans, that gives you so much honor and enlightening, *inshā'Allāh.* Shaykh Hisham Effendi is jewel; he knows such things and mostly when he is sleeping and speaking, and sleeping, dreaming. (Sweets) "I like to eat sweets, or sleep?" Yes sir, yes sir, yes sir.

Never ending, when you come to a feast, not able to eat everything. What is granted for you from the Divine Presence, you must take it and you must understand it. Alive people, they may eat and drink, but dead people, they are never asking to eat or to drink. O our Lord, don't make us to be dead ones, give us power from divine real life, to be forever in your Divine Presence, here and Hereafter!

Yā Rabbī, yā Rabbī akrimna, yā Rabbī mā akramt aʿibādika 's-sālihīn! Don't make our level the lowest level of donkeys!

May Allāh ﷻ forgive us.

Fātiḥah.

Fulfill the Lord's Orders with Love

Aʿūdhu billāhi min ash-Shaytāni 'r-rajīm. Biṣmillāhi 'r-Raḥmāni 'r-Raḥīm. Dastūr, yā Sayyidī. Madad, yā rijālAllāh!

Allāhu Akbar al-Akbar, Allāhu Akbar al-Akbar, Allāhu Akbar al-Akbar, Allāhu Akbar, Allāhu Akbar, Allāhu Akbar, lā ilāha illa-Llāh, Allāhu Akbar, Allāhu Akbar, wa lillāhi 'l-ḥamd! O our Lord! Give your most high glorifying and praising; You are not in need of such things. You may grant anyone that you created! You grant all praising and glory to Your most honored servant, Sayyidīna Muḥammad ﷺ!

Yā Rasūlullāh ﷺ! We are running to you and your shelter! You are *shafiʿ al-ummah,* Intercessor for all nations and all things! We are running under your holy flag, *liwa' l-ḥamd,* granted by your Lord to be always up, to the Day of Resurrection! You are calling all prophets and all *awlīyā* under your flag and they are coming with their nations and their followers. O our most beloved Prophet, Sayyidīna Muḥammad ﷺ! Countless salutes and *salāt* be upon you. Please, we are asking humbly for your intercession!

Allāhuma salli wa sallim ʿalā nabiyyina Muḥammad ʿalayhi 's-salām. Salātan tadūmu wahtūhda ilayh mammara 'l-layāli wa tūla 'd-dawām! Alfu salāt, alfu salām ʿalayka yā Sayyidi 'l-Awwalīn wa 'l-ʿĀkhirīn, yā Habībullāh! Allāh Allāh, Allāh Allāh. O Allāh, O Allāh! We are so weak ones, but we are foolishly brave. We are such no-mind ones, never thinking of our positions. *SubḥānAllāh, SulṭānAllāh!*

O our Listeners! Welcome to you, *as-salāmu ʿalaykum!* First we must ask from Quṭb az-Zamān, the Pole Saint of this planet, for a support to address all nations and all Mankind on this planet. And I am so weak, but if weak ones are supported by heavenly ones, they are most powerful from all Mankind. Even those who are proud of their nuclear weapons will be under my feet! But people think they are so powerful; no one is accepting to be a weak servant, to make his head humbly down. All of them are so proud, asking, "Who are you?!"

We were once in Daghestan, telling some stories about what is happening on Earth, millions or billions of happenings that give people a lesson to make them wake up. Because as Sayyidīna ʿAli ق, Allāh's blessing him, was saying, *an-nāsu niyāmun idha mātū intabahū,* "Human beings are asleep; when they die they awaken." No one knows his position or his station in the Divine Presence and heavenly level. It is important.

We may say first, *aʿūdhu billāhi min ash-Shaytāni 'r-rajīm,* to make our meeting not to go down by misunderstanding, as misunderstanding makes people down. But Shaytān is trying to make everyone understand something else; Shaytān has countless deceits and countless tricks and countless traps! Therefore, first of all you must say, *aʿūdhu billāhi min ash-Shaytāni 'r-rajīm.* "O our Lord we are running to You from that worst-mannered one among all Creation, Shaytān, that You threw away from the Divine Presence."

If someone is thrown away from the Divine Presence, if you are accepting and say, "Welcome to you," what is your position, how it will be? You are going on the same level as that Shaytān! Therefore, O Believers, beware from Shaytān! I am surprised people are writing on their fences, "Beware of Dog," and I am never seeing in any church or cathedral written on their doors, "Beware of Shaytān."

Beware Shaytān. What is that? Why they are not writing? They must write, according to the Holy Addressing from Heavens to holy ones. The Lord of Heavens is saying, "O My beloved ones. You are saying about Shaytān and you are My prophets, My messengers."

Are you not saying to them Shaytān is the most terrible and dangerous enemy for you? Why they are not writing this for you, "Beware Shaytān"? That is making people to fall down into nets. How you are not saying to them? They are not listening to us, but listening to Shaytān, deceiving themselves.

And they are very happy to follow Shaytān, but they are very upset if you are saying something about heavenly knowledge through heavenly messages. Their faces become so ugly! Who is accepting heavenly addressing to people and their hearts opening, will be dressed with lightening clothes. Therefore, look at the faces of Mankind. If you are seeing that his face makes you happy, you must understand that that one is *qābil,* accepting heavenly addressing. Therefore, that light comes on them and they will be enlightened ones. Whom their faces give you *nufūr*, hatred, you must understand that that person is with Shaytān and Shaytān is with him.

If their faces open with light, sometimes I am looking at people and saying, "*Māshā'Allāh,* you have so much light on your face," that person is trying to run away from Shaytān, asking to run to Heavens, and Allāh commands the angels, "Dress My servant with enlightened clothes," and his appearance is lightened. Therefore, their appearance is so sweet. You may look at them and your heart is getting in peace. But others' faces mixed with ugliness, run away from them because they are representatives of Shaytān. Shaytān is never laughing or smiling, and heavenly anger is always coming on him. Every second that he is not falling into *sajdah*, always, every second that heavenly anger is coming on him and dressing Shaytān with such an ugly appearance!

That is important, because every moment the Lord of Heavens looks at that one, to check if he is running to make *sajdah*. Allāh ﷻ says, "I am not accepting your *sajdah* to Me as long as you are not making *sajdah* to My beloved one!" The moment Shaytān may say, "O my Lord, I am making *sajdah*, what You have ordered to everyone. I am ready now to make *sajdah*," then the curse on him will be finished. That moment, he is going to be dressed with a heavenly enlightened suit. Finished! But no, Shaytān will not do that.

And Mankind also, who are running away from *sajdah*, running away from Allāh Almighty's Mercy Oceans, their faces are more dark, dark, dark, dark. We pray, "O our Lord, keep us not to be like Shaytān."

O People! Remember every moment that you are one servant from Mankind and try to give your servanthood to your Lord with an open heart. Make *sajdah* with love, pray with love, do everything that the Lord of Heavens orders you with love. Love carries love, and hatred carries hatred and darkness; who has that feels they are in a prison. If they are not in prison, they may go from east to west.

They say, "You can do everything for our treatment, and we are going to America, because Americans are on the top point for treating our illnesses." But that is not an illness. Illness belongs to your physical being, which is easily cured. But really people are hurt in their inner lives. That is a heavenly being you are imprisoning in yourself and not giving it freedom. In such a case, American doctors, Japanese doctors, Buddhist doctors or Jewish doctors cannot give you any cure.

O People! Don't think what you are making, "New Year celebration", is taking away from you everything you are carrying. It is only one moment that you are making yourself through a dark, dark position. For one minute you are making homes to be in darkness and in that darkness, a teaching of Shaytān cheats you. And you are thinking that one moment of sin is giving to all your life a pleasure. Never! You may awake in the morning and look at yourself, saying, "Now I am worse than I was last night. I thought I would finish problems in the first moment of the New Year and that my happiness would be forever!"

This warning is an ocean, but people are on the wrong way. They are not saying, *aʿūdhu billāhi min ash-Shaytāni 'r-rajīm* and they are not coming to *Bismillāhi 'r-Raḥmāni 'r-Raḥīm. Bismillāhi 'r-Raḥmāni 'r-Raḥīm* is the reins of your donkey. Cyprus donkeys are famous. If they like to learn something, buy them from here to teach all of them!

Anything not coming from our inside is an imitation! They are asking happiness from the New Year celebration. Shaytān makes them run in the streets and shout, "Yeeeooooh, ooooh, eeeeeh, eh ah!" One donkey lost its way and runs to look, "All people like me are shouting, 'Eeeeaaaaw! We are so happy tonight and waiting for darkness, because it brings us something only once a year," and we are kicking up and down!'"

That is *shaytānic* teaching to make people believe that happiness comes from outside. No, never! If coming from outside on the first night of the New Year makes you so happy, then why aren't you making it more and more and more? If you are finding so much happiness in darkness, so much pleasure and enjoyment, then repeat it! But they say, "No, if we are repeating, there is no more taste." They understand, but when they are drunk they are not understanding. When they are coming to themselves, they say, "Oh, what did we do last night? We lost so many things, we were thinking that happiness would come at midnight and we were asking to continue but now..."

Shaytān was ordered to make *sajdah* to Adam ﷺ, who is representing Allāh's deputy, and he refused to make *sajdah.* And the doors opened when that one made *sajdah,* carrying that one from troubles, miseries, badness, and dirtiness, and dressed him with endless pleasure and a crown put on his head that will only be for him, on his level, and no other. Shaytān's level can never be the level of Mankind; he is not from Mankind! That is an important point.

Why are you not saying such things, O Pope, O chief rabbi, oh *muftis* of Muslim countries! Why you are not speaking against New Year's celebrations? Allāh, the Lord of Heavens, will ask you why you are not warning and making your people wake up to know realities!

Allāh Almighty is looking to those who are worshipping, who are keeping His command and advising people on Truth. Why are you not making such a declaration for that night, that it belongs to Shaytān? No prophet allowed such a thing! If no prophet did it, how are they doing it? I'm asking Muslims first, then Christians, and then Jews. From where you are bringing this? Finding in the Old Testament, the New Testament? I Heavenly anger and heavenly revenge are approaching, because people are not following their prophets. They are not remembering to say, *Bismillāhi 'r-Raḥmāni 'r-Raḥīm, Lā ilāha illa-Llah, Lā ilāha illa-Llah, lā ilāha illa-Llāh.*

Shaykh Hisham Effendi, I am warning all holiness (leaders), they must declare realities for making people happy with them! Therefore, the Lord of Heavens is unhappy, and it is a not a good sign for His Holiness on the night of Christmas, to make him fall down. What does it mean? You may understand. The Lord of Heavens is not happy. Why you are not saying prophets' teachings?

This is what I am fighting. I am fighting Salafi *ʿulama* and doctors that are claiming, "We know something." You know something, but you are not declaring truth. Everywhere making candles, lights everywhere, for what, for Allāh or for Shaytān? I am asking Salafi *ʿulama* who are seeing their people also waiting, excited, waiting foe that night eagerly, to come so quickly. Why they are not awakening people? They know only to say *shirk, bidaʿ, kufr*! From which book they are saying this? And it is such an open subject, *man tashabbah bi-qawmin fa huwa minhum,* "Who imitates a people is from them." If Muslims are making themselves like non-Muslims, they will be like non-Muslims. *Allāh yantaqim minhum, Jala Jalālahu*!

I am nothing, but I have been ordered to speak to people from east to west. If understanding, they are saving themselves. If not understanding, then a heavenly punch is coming on them. That just happened before to so many nations; heavenly anger took them away. Now there is coming another heavenly anger! May Allāh protect *mu'mins,* protects believers, protects good ones, protects those who are running to Allāh and His beloved one.

O our Lord! Forgive us; we know nothing! Send us good ones who representing your prophets, to save us from Shaytān and *shaytanic* tricks, to not fall in Shaytān's trap.

O People! Keep yourselves in your homes. Recite Qur'an, and pray and ask forgiveness from Allāh Almighty in this holy month, Muharram al-Haram. And I am asking *duʿa* for you also that Allāh Almighty keeps you on His right track. O Allāh, forgive us! *Astaghfirullāh. Tawbah yā Rabbī,* I am weak, I am very, very weak one! Keep us on Your right path! We are saying throughout east and west:

Bismillāhi 'r-Raḥmāni 'r-Raḥīm. Bismillāhi 'Lladhī lā yadurru ma 'ismihī shayun fi 'l-ardi wa lā fi 's-samā' wa huwa 's-sami'u 'l-'alīm. Bismillāhi 'r-Raḥmāni 'r-Raḥīm.

May Allāh ﷻ forgive us.

Fātiḥah.

Prophet Holds Your Key

Aʿūdhu billāhi min ash-Shaytāni ʻr-rajīm. Biṣmillāhi ʻr-Raḥmāni ʻr-Raḥīm. Dastūr, yā Sayyidī. Madad, yā rijālAllāh!

Lā ilāha illa-Llāh, lā ilāha illa-Llāh, lā ilāha illa-Llāh Muḥammadun Rasūlullāh ʿalayhi salātullāh wa salām. Thumma as-salāmu ʿalayk Yā Sāhib al-Waqt, thumma as-salāmu ʿalayk Yā Sulṭān al-Awlīyā, thumma as-salātu wa ʻs-salāmu ʿalayk, yā Quṭb az-Zamān.

Welcome to you, our listeners. Welcome! Welcome, and we are saying, *aʿūdhu billāhi min ash-Shaytāni ʻr-rajīm. Bismillāhi ʻr-Raḥmāni ʻr-Raḥīm.* We must not be late. First we must say, *aʿūdhu billāhi min ash-Shaytāni ʻr-rajīm. Bismillāhi ʻr-Raḥmāni ʻr-Raḥīm.*

O People! Don't make your hearts occupied with useless things. Hear and listen! O our holy one, O our master, master of this planet, Quṭb az-Zamān, *quṭb ad-dunyā.* The pole star is never changing its position. At night, you are looking and finding it at the same point; during the daytime, the morning, early morning you may look at the pole star and it is in the same position. Eastern people are seeing that it is on the same position; Western people are seeing that the pole star is in the same position all the time.

When did time begin? Do you know? O our professors, do you know when time began? It is a very simple question. When did time begin? They are very proud ones; they know everything! Say, when did time begin and how did time begin? What is its beginning and what is going to be its end?

O People! listen. I am listening. I am not claiming that I am knowing something, no. But as our master for this planet is sending me some, not inspirations, coming from up to your instruments, yes, wavelength. If in material being and in material objects, there is going to be that connection, what about for our spiritual being; (does it not have) any connection with the Heavens? We have been granted such a position that the Lord of Heavens is saying, "I am going to bring a new generation, a new Creation, a new creature that I am granting to those ones, to be My deputies."

Think on it, think on it, O People! O we are saying *Bismillāhi ʻr-Raḥmāni ʻr-Raḥīm.* That is the key for opening every treasure, here and Hereafter. *Bismillāhi ʻr-Raḥmāni ʻr-Raḥīm.* If you are using *Bismillāhi ʻr-Raḥmāni ʻr-Raḥīm,* that opens for you what you are asking to be opened. If you are not saying *Bismillāhi 'r-Raḥmāni 'r-Raḥīm,* that can't be. If not only this world's people, if all the angels in the Heavens are coming and asking to turn that key for opening, they can't do it.

O Shaykh, what is behind that opening? What is there? Yes, now people are in their imitated bodies. Imitated, it is not our real being. This is not our real being. There is for everything a real being and there is a most-high position that any creature may reach for understanding of itself, that is just a closed curtain. If you are asking about yourself before you are asking about your Lord, you must ask about yourself, because your real being is behind that curtain and the imitated one is here. Our beings on this planet are imitated; it is not our real being. It can't be that anyone is carrying his real being and is on this planet.

O *ʿulama* of the Salafis, laughter once again! I am saying and you are not understanding or answering. Where was our Creator's *khitāb* (address)? When our Creator, the Lord of Heavens is asking people, "Mankind, who are you? Who am I? Who am I and who are you?" We answered, "You are our Lord, our Creator, and we are Your servants." That is our first oath that our real beings are hearing, looking and answering. Where did it happen? O Salafi *ʿulama,* what are they saying about where it happened, that our Lord is addressing whom, and what are they? We are saying to whom?

The Children of Adam, *dhurriyah*, Adam's generation, all of them are standing up. I am also asking the Salafi *ʿulama,* what do you think, that when the Lord of Heavens, our Creator, addressed our real beings, (did they) leave when they may be anywhere the Lord just appointed? I am asking about that one's *dharrah*, our souls, yes. The souls, what do you think: they were standing on their feet, sitting, or in *sajdah*? What was their position? A person who is praying to their Lord, are they standing up?

This is a very fine and very important real reality. The first is from hidden knowledge, they were first standing up. Then they are going not to continue standing up in the Divine Presence, when He was asking, "Who are you? Who am I?" They can't keep themselves standing up; they are coming to *rukʿū,* (bowing). In *khitāb,* heavenly addressing is coming to them. The third time, "Who are you? Who am I" They are finished and are running to *sajdah.*

How are they? Do they have an appearance, the same appearance or same positions for all? Our spiritual beings, were they all the same or with different appearances? Once they are teaching us now, the appearance on that day Allāh Almighty was creating and asking Man, "Who am I and who are you?" Yes, they are going, going, going and finishing, they are running in their Lord's Oceans. That ocean is giving our positions. It is giving our Creation in the holy command of Allāh Almighty. Don't think that what was on your right hand similar to me, or what is on the left hand is similar to the right hand. No, never. No one is seeing the same appearance. It is an ocean for Creation and each one from those creatures have a special looking point, a special understanding level, and a special enlightened direction for them in that ocean.

Allāhu Akbar, Allāhu Akbar, Allāhu Akbar! (Allāh is saying,) "You know nothing, you know nothing. We know something." That is so simple now because the time is over now and the Day of Resurrection is coming. Just such knowledge is going to be granted to living ones to understand something. You may be in that Divine Presence and your head's appearance is a heavenly appearance, to your head it is something else, what our bodies are looking at is something else, and downstairs it is something else. They are not in the same position, no. If it was the same for everything, then you will be like a piece of wood: there is nothing on it. But we have 360 different organs, yes? Each organ is taking something else according to their creation, according to their original position.

Therefore, they are sometimes making me ask some questions that no one can be able to know by reading books. This is because such knowledge is running from the Heavens to pure hearts and pure hearts have a special cleanliness, a special understanding. Your eyes understand something and your ears understand something else. The 360 different organs, each one must take their positions on that line, they must move.

I am asking Salafi *ʿulama* if people have feet, body organs, or what was it? This being, O Salafi *ʿulama,* is it much more important than that being? This being has a material appearance, it can't carry for any second to be that appearance. Our spiritual being, you can't understand; we have it but we can't understand it. Do you think the car can understand its motor? No. Do you have a motor for yourself or are you empty? There is a heart, it is a piece of meat. This flesh knows everything? No. It only knows about its *muhimmah.* Its job is nothing else. It is sending blood from the center of life to the whole body, to every cell; that is its importance. But when the blood is running and reaching up to the last point of our physical being, its blood also does not know what they are doing or what is happening. When they are carrying the blood to organs, they do not know what is happening; they are only bringing blood to every organ. But what is its position? It doesn't know.

Therefore, the most important and honored creatures are the Children of Adam. Adam (as) is not looking according to his physical being, no. What is carrying it, our physical being? It is not. But the real reality is that the blood is running and reaching every cell. It is just different, as for everything there is something, some mission, some importance to make it up to its perfection. But people are not trained to know such special knowledge. They know from the Heavens and the Heavens are sending such knowledge in your holy books to special ones on this planet, and they are asking to give everything. If it is right, they know it. Therefore, we are saying to the Pole and the Pole may ask the Lord of Heavens. The Lord is asking all Mankind, "Who am I and who are you?" Every spot of our blood is reaching one cell and is asking it, "Do you know from where this power is coming to you?" Every cell is making a *sajdah*, prostration, answering, "You, our Lord, are sending to us. We are looking to You, not what blood is sending to us!"

O People! Try to understand something about spirituality. It is more important for you to look after that than your physical being. To enjoy your physical being is the level of animals. Your level is over the level of angels. How are you making yourself down, down? You are getting so proud and enjoying yourself with such things.

Why are you not looking up? You are always looking at the Earth and sometimes, O Shaykh, we are looking at what is happening in the skies in space.

Yes, we know there are so many billions of stars around the sun and we are looking and not understanding. The Lord of Heavens is never making something that you can't understand but, we are not using our power to know about ourselves. Therefore, the first question on the Day of Resurrection will be, "What have you learned?" Look! How are you going to reply, or how are you answering? Who is asking that question? What are you going to say? "O our Lord, we were busy with our business and there was no time for us to find an empty time to look at what is happening in space." Leave your looking! (It is) nothing, but what is in Heavens is written and Mankind has been informed by some special ones, whose beings are special beings, *hazrati insān* (revered Mankind). Man has been honored to be the master of this life. Why are you not going to learn from them? You are not going to learn by saying, "We are thinking;" thinking is not going to open realities to you. You will look for keys that have been granted to prophets. That key-keeper is your Prophet ﷺ and you are looking to another?

They are saying, "What is that? What is that?" That is, that we are living on the first level of our material being. When we are asking for more for spirituality, it is enough to carry us up, up, up, to the first level, second level, third level, fourth, fifth level, sixth level and seventh level. When you are asking, angels may carry you up to Sidratu 'l-Muntaha (the Lote-tree of the Utmost Boundary). That is the last point of material beings. Up (above that), you can't know until you clean yourself:

wa thiyābaka fathahhir

And your garments do purify. *74:4*

One meaning, it is to clean your soul from every material aspect and come. We are dressing you with another dress that you may improve, up and up with these clothes. The dressing on Earth is always dirty. Clean it and then angels are coming and taking that dirty dressing from you, and dressing you in such a dress that you can move in those enlightened stations, one after one. You may improve in levels endlessly.

O People! Don't waste your time so much! You may be asking or working a little bit to reach something beyond this material world. We are looking only to material beings and we are not asking what is behind our material being. People, all of them have just occupied themselves in these material oceans, not anything else behind this. Therefore, now, people time after time are not being able to taste something from spirituality and they are saying, "We are not interested in anything beyond our material life." This It means that person is asking to stay always in the WC (water closet/bathroom), and the Lord of Heavens is saying, "Clean yourself. Don't use the WC so much. Clean yourself, if you are asking to come to Me."

The whole world is like a WC. Nothing is given, but from material being it is finishing. And when the curtains from his eyes are opening, he will say, "If we were trying to reach something from that level, it will be best for us." Nothing is being given to people for their real beings. They are being made to run after it, to be in trouble, finished! When you are finishing, eyes opening and you are saying, "Oh! If we were trying to reach something from those levels, will be best for us."

O People! Beware not to fall in dark holes, black holes; try to reach white and brilliant holes so that you can be so happy and have endlessly enjoyment for yourself. You are reaching brilliant white holes and you are never going to be tired for your actions there. Try not to be tired here or

Hereafter, to have your last station be enlightened positions. May Allāh forgive us, and blessings for you.

O People! Sometimes they are speaking on such things that if we are understanding one word, it is going to be a key for opening other positions of our beings on this planet. May Allāh forgive us!

O our Lord! We know nothing. In this holy month, send us from darkness into enlightened territories to Your Heavenly Oceans.

Whoever is accepting they may reach such a level in all Heavens, directing people to some aspects that they like to reach it.

May Allāh ﷻ forgive us.

Fātiḥah.

The First Command Is to Be Clean Ones

Allāhu Akbar, Allāhu Akbar, lā ilāha illa-Llāh, Allāhu Akbar, Allāhu Akbar, wa lillāhi 'l-ḥamd! Alfu salāt, alfu salām ʿalayka wa ʿalā ālika yā Sayyidīna yā Rasūlullāh, yā Habībullāh narju shafaʿatak yā Sayyidi 'l-Awwalīn wa 'l-ʿĀkhirīn. Aʿūdhu billāhi min ash-Shaytāni 'r-rajīm. Bismillāhi 'r-Raḥmāni 'r-Raḥīm.

O Mankind! Welcome and blessings on you, who are taking a care for hearing, for learning, and for granting all their praises and glorification according to their possibility. Allāh grants you from His endless blessing oceans. First of all, He is asking that we must be clean, *tahir thiyabaka.*

wa thiyabaka fattahir.

And keep your garment free from stain. *74:4*

First of all the Lord of Heavens is sending His Holy command through His most holiest one, to all prophets and their nations. First, He is asking that His deputies must be clean ones. If they are not cleaning themselves then it is impossible to be granted to those people who are not coming cleanly. Cleanliness is the first command from the beginning up to the end. Allāh Almighty is never accepting a dirty one. He is saying you must be clean. No one can go to a king's presence with dirty clothes nor can one ask to be seen in a king's presence with an ugly appearance, yes. Everyone is asking to be the most clean and good looking one in that assembly. Therefore, we must try to be clean ones.

O our Listeners! don't listen to me, but the master of this planet, according to His holy commands is asking us to be clean ones. We were in school, schoolboys and our school master was making our hands like this on the desk. When he was looking at our nails, which were not clean. He was making like this (hits) and looking also at our ears if they were clean or not. Look, what about that you are you asking to go to the Heavenly Presence of the Lord of the Heavens? *Astaʿidhu billāh.*

W'Allāhu yadʿū ilā dāri 's-salām.

But Allāh does call to the Home of Peace. *10:25*

O our Salafi *ʿulama,* why are you not telling people to look at their nails, to look at their cleanliness? Why are you not ordering and I am asking his

Holiness the Pope if he is ordering Christians, Catholics or Orthodox or Protestant to be clean? Why are they not giving this command? A clean one is going to be well known when his dead body is put in the *kaffan*. You may understand if he is clean or not. If a bad smell is coming from his dead body that means he is not clean.

Once when I was in Damascus, the government asked to build a wider road to make transportation easier, because there were so many cars and it was impossible to move the traffic. They were asking to take away some buildings to make a large way, a wider boulevard for traffic. On that way there was a saint, who was lying in his tomb for 600 years. They were forcing people to give permission so that they could take a grand *walī's* body from his *maqām*, to a further place. That grand *walī* wasn't happy to be taken from his first tomb to another place, for two reasons. One reason was, he wasn't asking for his body to be shown. Some people are in their graves and their flesh is finishing. *Awlīyā* are never like that. They are not a skeleton and they know this and are keen not to have their miraculous bodies be seen by anyone. The government forced that.

Once before that event, perhaps 40 years ago, at the time of the French government, the high commissioner in Syria ordered that this tomb must be taken away. At night, Shaykh Hasan was coming to that one, saying, "Are you saying that you must take my grave from here? Not you, not your country, the soldiers, or all your people can take me from here!" In the morning they said, "No one is touching that one." *Karāmatu 'l-awlīyā haqq*, "The miracles of saints are real (Article of Faith)."

O Salafi *ʿulama*! You must believe this and say this, *karāmatu 'l-awlīyā haqq*. The miracles of *awlīyā* are a grant from Allāh Almighty to them. You must believe that happened.

The second time, that French high commissioner was leaving Syria in the hands of Syrians. Much more traffic was coming and they were asking the descendants of Shaykh Hasan Jibawi, *hadrati ʿala Allāhu taʿala darajātihi dā'iman, yā Sayyidī dastūr. bī idhnAllāh*, you may hear.

O Salafi *ʿulama*! You must believe in *karāmatu 'l-awlīyā*. If not, I don't like to make anything for you, but those who are appointed to keep the honor of *anbīyā* and *awlīyā* may touch you. They are not sending you bombs or bullets; one small creature may touch you at night and by morning people are coming to take your dead body!

Fear Allāh. Don't speak against *awlīyā*. Don't think that now you can find *awlīyā*, as before this time they were hiding themselves. Therefore, you ordered to destroy everything in Jannatu 'l-Muʿala and Jannatu 'l-Baqī'. But now it is not the same time and you must fear. At least two *jinns* may take your body, one from one ear and the other from the second ear, and put you in a desert until you pass away.

Fear Allāh ﷻ! He is not looking at such a thing. But on behalf of the Seal of Prophets, there is another *tajalli,* a manifestation now, that may touch (you.) The manifestations have just changed from the beginning of this Muharram. You are hearing that in Iran, there are so many troubles. Before, people were not doing anything and they were peaceful. But now, they are standing up and saying, "We are asking to do what we like, we are not people like our ancestors before us who were saying, 'O yes sir, we are not saying (anything) now.' If you are seeing anything wrong, now we are coming in front of you. We are asking our rights. We are not accepting your system, we want the system that the Lord of the Heavens sent to us. We are a hundred million Iranians here not just one person asking to do as he likes. You must listen to us. We are not happy with you because you are not going on the right way and the Lord of Heavens is seeing what you are doing."

You are only in two breaths one up, one down. Fear Allāh, O our leaders. Come to *shari'atullāh,* Allāh Almighty's order. Now, therefore, time has just changed from the beginning of this Muharram, 1431. It is never going to be the same as before. Everything is going to be changed according to the holy command of the Heavens. *Allāhu Akbar, awlīyāullāh, Allāh,* keep their respect.

O Wahabis! It is not easy now to take people away from visiting tombs of *awlīyā* and *anbīyā.* Take care on this point. Be careful. This is a warning coming from the Heavens. Don't look to me; you must think, who is warning you? All prophets are coming as warners. Those who are taking care will be saved and those who are not taking care will be taken away. Don't say who is that one? I am nothing. You may understand the power that runs in my heart after a while, but it will be too late.

At the time, the descendants of Shaykh Hasan Jibawi, a grand *walī,* prayed for three days and three nights on his minaret:

As-salāt was-salām ʿalayka, yā Rasūlullāh!
As-salāt was-salām ʿalayka, yā Habībullah!
As-salāt was-salām ʿalayka, yā Nabīullah!
As-salāt was-salām ʿalayka, yā Nūru 'l-Arshillāh!

Then *sakīnah* (tranquility) coming. Satisfaction and peacefulness was coming after three days and three nights. His last descendant understood that Grandshaykh was giving permission to be taken away. I was there that day and they were opening and finding his body. Allāh and His *Rasūl* are witnesses, the *awlīyā* of Sham are witnesses. When they were looking at what was happening and they opened his grave, there was a beautiful smell coming. The shaykh was as if sleeping, his body as it was before and his beard just like my beard now. He was lying and his descendant put his hand under his head, saying, "O my grandfather, O *walīullāh,* that is *ūlu 'l-amr,* their order."

His coffin was white, not gray, like wheat fully grown, and no longer green, but yellow. Taking him out and putting in a new coffin. People were saying, *Allāhuma salli ʿalā Sayyidīna Muḥammad, Allāhuma salli ʿalā Sayyidīna Muḥammad.* People were running to reach his coffin. Even with their fingers they couldn't reach. From this place up to the mosque it was two hours away. Crowds of Muslims were going around the coffin and at ʿAsr time he was put in his new *maqām.*

I was living there at that time, and after ten days I was taking something for a needy family. I passed and some children came running after me with soil in their hands, saying, "O Shaykh, smell it." It was the perfume of rose. They were bringing it after ten days from where he was lying for 500 years. *SubḥānAllāh,* I am a witness. *Inshā'Allāh,* I am not lying to you, that is a clean one.

There are so many people that are dirty ones. I was burying some of them. When you are standing for praying, their dirty smell is coming. We were putting them in the grave, people were quickly covering the dirty smell. I was also witness. So many times I was burying people and when a dirty smell was coming, I am asking from where? It was coming from that grave, and that dirtiness, and dirty smell is not finishing. For some of them it is for 40 days, for some of them 40 years.

Look, O *ʿulama,* you must teach people, the first command of Allāh Almighty is to clean yourself and come. "First ablution and then come to Me." But now, people are not thinking on it and all *ʿulama* or particularly doctors, they are never taking any care to wake people up. Mostly they are under the command of governments. No, governments must listen and obey real *ʿulama.* That is the holy command and they are not doing and punishment is running on them.

O People! Try to be clean. The first command of Allāh Almighty is, "Be clean and come to Me clean. Come to My Divine Presence clean and you will be saved. Those who are dirty with *dunyā,* they are thrown away from the Divine Presence."

O People! It is a very important command that they are making me speak on. Dirtiness is making the biggest trouble for Mankind now because they are not clean. All trouble from east to west and from north to south because they are dirty ones. Be clean ones. Today you are here. Tomorrow you are not. Be clean. May Allāh ﷻ forgive us.

O People! O our Lord for the honor of this holy night from *Shahr* Muharram al-Harām, for the honor of the most beloved one in Your Presence, forgive us and bless us and send us someone that may take us from dirtiness to cleanliness. O our Lord! Send us someone who is going to destroy the Kingdom of Shaytān and Shaytāns.

Allāh Allāh, Allāh Allāh, Allāh Allāh, Dā'im Allāh, Dā'im Allāh!
SubḥānAllāh, Sulṭān Allāh, SubḥānAllāh, Sulṭān Allāh!

May Allāh ﷻ forgive us.

Fātiḥah.

Islamic Calendar and Holy Days

The Islamic calendar is lunar-based, with twelve months of 29 or 30 days and a year of 354 days. A lunar year is shorter than a solar year, so Muslim holy days cycle back in the Gregorian (Western) calendar. This is how, for example, Ramaḍān is celebrated at different times of the year, as the annual Islamic calendar is ten days shorter than the Gregorian calendar.

Four months are sacred, in which war is prohibited, unless Muslims are attacked and must defend themselves: Muharram, Rajab, Dhūl-Qᶜadah and Dhūl-Hijjah. Holy months include "God's Month" (Rajab), "Prophet's Month" (Shaᶜbān) and the "Month of the People" (Ramaḍān), in which pious acts are rewarded more generously.

Months of the Islamic Calendar

Muḥarram	Rajab
Safar	Shaᶜbān
Rabīᶜ ul-Awwal (Rabīᶜ I)	Ramaḍān
Rabīᶜ uth-Thāni (Rabīᶜ II)	Shawwāl
Jumāda al-Awwal (Jumādi I)	Dhū'l-Qᶜadah
Jumāda uth-Thāni (Jumādi II)	Dhū'l-Hijjah

al-Hijrah

The 1st of Muharram marks the beginning of the Islamic New Year, chosen because it is the anniversary of Prophet Muḥammad's ﷺ historic *hijrah* (migration) from Mecca to Madinah, where he established the first, preeminent Muslim community in which he introduced unprecedented social reforms, including civil law, human and women's rights, religious tolerance, taxation to serve the community, and military ethics.

ᶜAshura

On 10th Muharram, ᶜAshūra commemorates many sacred events, such as Noah's ark coming to rest, the birth of Abraham, and the building of the Kaᶜbah in Mecca. ᶜAshūra is a major holy day, marked with two days of fasting, on the $9^{th}/10^{th}$ or on $10^{th}/11^{th}$ based on a holy tradition (*hadīth*) of Sayyidīna Muḥammad ﷺ.

Mawlid

Mawlid al-Nabī, 12th Rabiʿ al-Awwal, commemorates Prophet Muḥammad's birth in 570. Mawlid is celebrated globally throughout this month in huge communal gatherings in which a famous poem "Qasīdah al-Burdah" is recited, accompanied by drummers, illustrious poetry recitals, religious singing, eloquent sermons, gift giving, feasts, and feeding the poor. Most Muslim nations observe Mawlid as a national holiday.

Laylat al-Isra wal-Mi'raj

Literally, "the Night Journey and Ascension;" 27th of Rajab is when Sayyidīna Muḥammad ﷺ physically traveled from Mecca to Jerusalem, ascended in all the levels of Heaven from a rock in the Dome of the Rock, and returned to Mecca—while his bed was still warm. In the Night Journey, Islam's five daily prayers were ordained by God. Sayyidīna Muḥammad ﷺ also prayed with Abraham, Moses, and Jesus in Jerusalem's al-Aqsa Mosque, signifying that Muslims, Christians, and Jews follow one god. This holy event designated Jerusalem as the third holiest site in Islam, after Mecca and Madinah.

Laylat al-Bara'ah

The "Night of Freedom from Fire" occurs on 15th Shaʿbān. On this night God's Mercy is great; hence, the night is spent reciting Holy Qur'an and special prayers, as well as visiting the deceased.

Ramadan

Many regard Ramaḍān, the 9th month of the Islamic calendar, the holiest month of the year. Muslims observe a strict fast and participate in pious activities such as charitable giving and peace making. It is a time of intense spiritual renewal for those who observe it. Fasting is meant to instill social awareness of the needy, and to promote gratitude for God's endless favors. The fast is typically broken in a communal setting, and hence Ramaḍān is a highly social month. At night, a special Ramaḍān prayer known as "Tarawīh" is offered in congregation, in which one-thirtieth of the Holy Qur'an is recited by the *imām* (prayer leader); thus the entire holy book of 6,000 verses is recited in this month.

Eid al-Fitr

"Festival of Fast-Breaking" marks the end of Ramaḍān and is celebrated the first three days of Shawwāl. It is a time for charity and celebration with family and friends for completing a month of blessings and joy. In the Last Days of Ramaḍān, each Muslim family gives "Zakāt al-Fitr"(charity of fast-breaking) which consists of cash and/or food, to help the poor. On the first early morning of Eid, Muslims observe a special congregational prayer, such as Christmas/Easter Mass or the High Holy Days. After Eid prayer is a time to visit family and friends, and give gifts and money (especially to children). Many specialty foods and sweets are prepared solely for Eid days. In most Muslim countries, the entire three days of Eid is a national holiday.

Yawm al-Arafat

"Day of ʿArafat," the 9th Dhul-Hijjah, occurs just before the celebration of Eid al-Adha. Pilgrims on Hajj assemble for the "standing" on the plain of ʿArafat, located outside Mecca, where they contemplate the Day of Standing (Resurrection Day). Muslims elsewhere in the world fast this day, and gather at a local mosque for prayers. Thus, those who cannot perform Hajj that year still honor the sacrifice of Abraham.

Eid al-Adha

The "Feast of Sacrifice," celebrated from the 10th-13th Dhul-Hijjah, marks Prophet Abraham's willingness to sacrifice his son Ismaʿil on God's order. To honor this event, Muslims perform Hajj, the pilgrimage to Mecca that is incumbent on every mature Muslim once in their life if they have the means. Celebrations begin with an animal sacrifice to commemorate Sayyidīna Abraham's sacrifice. In Islam, he is known as *Khalīlullāh*, "God's friend." Many consider him the first Muslim and a premiere role model, for his obedience to God and willingness to sacrifice his only child without even questioning the command.

Glossary

ʿabd (pl. *ʿibād*): lit. slave, servant.
ʿAbdAllāh: Lit., "servant of God"
Abū Bakr aṣ-Ṣiddīq: the closest Companion of Prophet Muḥammad; the Prophet's father-in-law, who shared the *Hijrah* with him. After the Prophet "s death, he was elected the first caliph (successor); known as one of the most saintly Companions.
Abū Yazīd/Bayāzīd Bistāmī: A great ninth century *walī* and a master of the Naqshbandi Golden Chain.
adab: good manners, proper etiquette.
adhān: call to prayer.
Ākhirah: the Hereafter; afterlife.
al-: Arabic definite article, "the"
ʿalāmīn: world; universes.
Alḥamdūlillāh: praise God.
ʿAlī ibn Abī Ṭālib: first cousin of Prophet Muḥammad, married to his daughter Fāṭimah; the fourth caliph.
alif: first letter of Arabic alphabet.
ʿAlīm, al-: the Knower, a divine attribute
Allāh: proper name for God in Arabic.
Allāhu Akbar: God is Greater.
ʿāmal: good deed (pl. *ʿamāl*).
amīr (pl., *umarā*): chief, leader, head of a nation or people.
anā: first person singular pronoun
anbīyā: prophets (sing. *nabī*).
ʿaql: intellect, reason; from the root *ʿaqila*: lit., "to fetter."
ʿArafah, ʿArafat: a plain near Mecca where pilgrims gather for the principal rite of Hajj.
ʿarif: knower, Gnostic; one who has reached spiritual knowledge of his Lord.
ʿĀrifūnʿ bil-Lāh: knowers of God.
Ar-Raḥīm: The Mercy-Giving, Merciful, Munificent, one of Allāh's ninety-nine Holy Names.
Ar-Raḥmān: The Most Merciful, Compassionate, Beneficent; the most repeated of Allāh's Holy Names.
ʿarsh, al-: the Divine Throne.
aṣl: root, origin, basis.
astāghfirullāh: lit. "I seek Allāh's forgiveness."
Awlīyāullāh: saints of Allāh (sing. *walī*).
āyah/āyāt (pl. *Ayāt*): a verse of the Holy Qur'an.
Āyat al-Kursī: "Verse of the Throne,"a well-known supplication from the Qur'an (2:255).
ʿAzraʿīl: the Archangel of Death.
Badīʿ al-: The Innovator; a divine name.
Banī Ādam: Children of Adam; humanity.
Bayt al-Maqdis: the Sacred Mosque in Jerusalem, built at the site where Solomon's Temple was later erected.
Bayt al-Maʿmūr: much-frequented house; this refers to the Kaʿbah of the Heavens, which is the prototype of the Kaʿbah on Earth, circumambulated by the angels.
bayaʿ: pledge; in the context of this book, the pledge of initiation of a disciple (*murīd*) to a shaykh.
Bismillāhi'r-Raḥmāni'r-Raḥīm: "In the name of the All-Merciful, the All-Compassionate"; introductory verse to all chapters of the Qur'an, except the ninth.
Dajjāl: the False Messiah (Anti-Christ) will appear at the end-time of this

world, who will deceive Mankind with false divinity.
dalālah: evidence.
dhāt: self / selfhood.
dhawq (pl. *adhwāq*): tasting; technical term referring to the experiential aspect of gnosis.
dhikr: remembrance, mention of God in His Holy Names or phrases of glorification.
ḍīyā: light.
Diwān al-Awlīyā: the nightly gathering of saints with Prophet Muḥammad in the spiritual realm.
du'a: supplication.
dunyā: world; worldly life.
'Eid: festival; the two major celebrations of Islam are 'Eid al-Fitr, after Ramaḍān; and 'Eid al-Adha, the Festival of Sacrifice during the time of Hajj, which commemorates the sacrifice of Prophet Abraham.
farḍ: obligatory worship.
Fātiḥah: Sūratu 'l-Fātiḥah; the opening chapter of the Qur'an.
Ghafūr, al-: The Forgiver; one of the Holy Names of God.
ghawth: lit. "Helper"; the highest rank of all saints.
ghaybu' l-muṭlaq, al-: the Absolute Unknown; known only to God.
ghusl: full shower/bath obligated by a state of ritual impurity, performed before worship.
Grandshaykh: generally, a *walī* of great stature. In this text, where spelled "Grandshaykh," refers to Mawlana 'Abd Allāh ad-Daghestani (d. 1973), Mawlana Shaykh Nazim's master.
hā': the Arabic letter ه
ḥadīth Nabawī (pl., *aḥadīth*): prophetic *ḥadīth* whose meaning and linguistic expression are those of Prophet Muḥammad.
Ḥadīth Qudsī: divine saying whose meaning directly reflects the meaning God intended but whose linguistic expression is not divine speech as in the Qur'an.
ḥaḍr: present
Hajj: the sacred pilgrimage of Islam obligatory on every mature Muslim once in their life.
ḥalāl: permitted, lawful according to Islamic *Shari'ah.*
ḥaqīqah, al-: reality of existence; ultimate truth.
ḥaqq: truth
Ḥaqq, al-: the Divine Reality, one of the 99 divine names.
ḥarām: forbidden, unlawful.
ḥasanāt: good deeds.
hāshā: God forbid.
ḥarf: (pl. *ḥurūf*) letter; Arabic root "edge."
Ḥawā: Eve.
ḥaywān: animal.
Hijrah: emigration.
ḥikmah: wisdom.
ḥujjah: proof.
hūwa: the pronoun "he," made up of the Arabic letters *hā'* and *wāw* .
'ibādu 'l-Lāh: servants of God.
'ifrīt: a type of Jinn, huge and powerful.
iḥsān: doing good, "It is to worship God as though you see Him; for if you are not seeing Him, He sees you."
ikhlāṣ, al-: sincere devotion.
ilāh: (pl. *āliha*): idols or gods.
ilāhīyya: divinity.
ilhām: divine inspiration sent to *awlīyāullāh*.
'ilm: knowledge, science.
'ilmu 'l-awrāq: knowledge of papers.
'ilmu 'l-adhwāq: knowledge of taste.
'ilmu 'l-ḥurūf: science of letters.

'ilmu 'l-kalām: scholastic theology.
'ilmun ladunnī: divinely inspired knowledge.
imān: faith, belief.
imām: leader of congregational prayer; an advanced scholar followed by a large community.
insān: humanity; pupil of the eye.
insānu 'l-kāmil, al-: the Perfect Man, *i.e.*, Prophet Muḥammad.
irādatullāh: the Will of God.
irshād: spiritual guidance.
ism: name.
isma-Llāh: name of God.
isrā': night journey; used here in reference to the night journey of Prophet Muḥammad.
Isrā'fīl: Archangel Rafael, in charge of blowing the Final Trumpet.
jalāl: majesty.
jamāl: beauty.
jama'a: group, congregation.
Jannah: Paradise.
jihad: to struggle in God's Path.
Jibrīl: Gabriel, Archangel of revelation.
Jinn: a species of living beings created from fire, invisible to most humans. Jinn can be Muslims or non-Muslims.
Jumu'ah: Friday congregational prayer, held in a large mosque.
Ka'bah: the first House of God, located in Mecca, Saudi Arabia to which pilgrimage is made and to which Muslims face in prayer.
kāfir: unbeliever.
Kalāmullāh al-Qadīm: lit., Allāh's Ancient Words, *viz.* the Holy Qur'an.
kalīmat at-tawḥīd: lā ilāha illa-Llāh: "There is no god but Al-Lah (the God)."
karāmat: miracles.
khalīfah: deputy.
Khāliq, al-: the Creator, one of 99 divine names.
khalq: Creation.
khāniqah: designated smaller place for worship other than a mosque; *zāwiyah.*
khuluq: conduct, manners.
Kirāmun Kātabīn: honored Scribe angels.
lā: no; not; not existent; the particle of negation.
lā ilāha illa-Llāh Muḥammadun Rasūlullāh: there is no deity except Allāh, Muḥammad is the Messenger of Allāh.
lām: Arabic letter ل.
al-Lawḥ al-*Maḥfūẓ*: the Preserved Tablets.
Laylat al-Isrā' wa'l-Mi'rāj: the Night Journey and Ascension of Prophet Muḥammad to Jerusalem and to the Seven Heavens.
Madīnātu 'l-Munawwara: the Illuminated city; city of Prophet Muḥammad; Madinah.
mahr: dowry, given by the groom to the bride.
malakūt: divine kingdom.
Malik, al-: the Sovereign, a divine name.
Mālik: Archangel of Hell.
maqām: spiritual station; tomb of a prophet, messenger or saint.
ma'rifah: gnosis.
Māshā'Allāh: as Allāh Wills.
Mawlānā: lit. "Our master" or "our patron,"referring to an esteemed person.
maẓhar: place of disclosure.
miḥrāb: prayer niche.
Mikā'īl: Michael, Archangel of rain.
mīzān: the scale that weighs our deeds on Judgment Day.
mīm: Arabic letter م.

minbar: pulpit.
Miracles: of *awlīyā*, known as *karamāt*; of prophets, known as *mu'jizāt* (lit., "That which renders powerless or helpless").
mi'rāj: the ascension of Prophet. Muḥammad from Jerusalem to the Seven Heavens.
Muḥammadun rasūlu 'l-Lāh: Muḥammad is the Messenger of God.
mulk, al-: the World of dominion.
Mu'min, al-: Guardian of Faith, one of the 99 Names of God.
mu'min: a believer.
munājāt: invocation to God in a very intimate form.
Munkir: one of the angels of the grave.
murīd: disciple, student, follower.
murshid: spiritual guide; *pir*.
mushāhadah: direct witnessing.
mushrik (pl. *mushrikūn*): idolater; polytheist.
muwwāḥid (pl. *muwāḥḥidūn*): those who affirm God's Oneness.
nabī: a prophet of God.
nāfs: lower self, ego.
Nakīr: the other angel of the grave (with Munkir).
nūr: light.
Nūḥ: the prophet Noah.
Nūr, an-: "The Source of Light"; a divine name.
Qādir, al-: "The Powerful"; a divine name.
qalam, al-: the Pen.
qiblah: direction, specifically, the direction faced by Muslims during prayer and other worship, towards the Sacred House in Mecca.
Quddūs, al-: "The Holy One"; a divine name.
qurb: nearness
quṭb (pl. *aqṭāb*): axis or pole. Among the poles are:
Quṭbu 'l-Bilād: Pole of the Lands.
Quṭbu 'l-Irshād: Pole of Guidance.
Quṭbu 'l-Aqṭāb: Pole of Poles.
Quṭbu 'l-A'dham: Highest Pole.
Quṭbu 'l-Mutasarrif: Pole of Affairs.
al-quṭbīyyatu 'l-kubrā: the highest station of poleship.
Rabb, ar-: the Lord.
Raḥīm, ar-: "The Most Compassionate"; a divine name.
Raḥmān, ar-: "The All-Merciful"; a divine name.
raḥmā: mercy.
raka'at: one full set of prescribed motions in prayer. Each prayer consists of a one or more *raka'ats.*
Ramaḍān: the ninth month of the Islamic calendar; month of fasting.
Rasūl: a messenger of God.
Rasūlullāh: the Messenger of God, Muḥammad ﷺ.
Ra'ūf, ar-: "The Most Kind"; a divine name.
Razzāq, ar-: "The Provider"; a divine name.
rawḥānīyyah: spirituality; spiritual essence of something.
Riḍwān: Archangel of Paradise.
rizq: provision; sustenance.
rūḥ: spirit. *Ar-Rūḥ* is the name of a great angel.
rukū': bowing posture of the prayer.
ṣadaqah: voluntary charity.
Saḥābah (sing., *saḥābi*): Companions of the Prophet; the first Muslims.
ṣaḥīḥ: authentic; term certifying validity of a ḥadīth of the Prophet.
ṣāim: fasting person (pl. *ṣāimūn*)
sajda (pl. *sujūd*): prostration.
ṣalāt: ritual prayer, one of the five obligatory pillars of Islam. Also, to invoke blessing on the Prophet.

Ṣalāt an-Najāt: prayer of salvation, offered in the late hours of night.
ṣalawāt (sing. *ṣalāt*): invoking blessings and peace upon the Prophet.
salām: peace.
Salām, as-: "The Peaceful"; a divine name. *As-salāmu ʿalaykum:* "Peace be upon you." (Islamic greeting).
Ṣamad, aṣ-: Self-Sufficient, upon whom creatures depend.
ṣawm, ṣiyām: fasting.
Sayāt: bad deeds.
sayyid: leader; also, a descendant of Prophet Muḥammad.
Sayyidīnā: our master (fem. *sayyidunā; sayyidatunā*: our mistress).
shahādah: lit. testimony; the testimony of Islamic faith: *Lā ilāha illa ʾl-Lāh wa Muḥammadun rasūlu ʾl-Lāh*, "There is no god but Allāh, the One God, and Muḥammad is the Messenger of God."
Shah Naqshband: Muḥammad Bahauddin Shah Naqshband, a great eighth century walī, and the founder of the Naqshbandi Ṭarīqah.
shaykh: lit. "old Man,"a religious guide, teacher; master of spiritual discipline.
shifāʿ: cure.
shirk: polytheism, idolatry, ascribing partners to God
ṣiffāt: attributes; term referring to Divine Attributes.
Silsilat adh-dhahabīyya: "Golden Chain"of spiritual authority in Islam
sohbet (Arabic, *suḥbah*): association: the assembly or discourse of a shaykh.
subḥānAllāh: glory be to God.
sulṭān/sulṭānah: ruler, monarch.
Sulṭān al-Awlīyā: lit., "King of the *awlīyā*; the highest-ranking saint.
Sūnnah: Practices of Prophet Muḥammad in actions and words; what he did, said, recommended, or approved of in his Companions.
sūrah: a chapter of the Qur'an; picture, image.
Sūratu ʾl-Ikhlāṣ: Chapter 114 of Holy Qur'an; the Chapter of Sincerity.
ṭabīb: doctor.
tābiʿīn: the Successors, one generation after the Prophet's Companions.
tafsīr: to explain, expound, explicate, or interpret; technical term for commentary or exegesis of the Holy Qur'an.
tajallī (pl. *tajallīyāt*): theophanies, God's self-disclosures, Divine Self-manifestation.
takbīr: lit. *"Allāhu Akbar,"*God is Great.
tarawīḥ: the special nightly prayers of Ramaḍān.
ṭarīqat/tarīqah: lit., way, road or path. An Islamic order or path of discipline and devotion under a guide or shaykh; Sufism.
tasbīḥ: recitation glorifying or praising God.
tawāḍaʿ: humbleness.
ṭawāf: the rite of circumambulating the Kaʿbah while glorifying God during Hajj and ʿUmra.
tawḥīd: unity; universal or primordial Islam, submission to God, as the sole Master of destiny and ultimate Reality.
Tawrāt: Torah
tayammum: Alternate ritual ablution performed in the absence of water.
ʿubūdīyyah: state of worshipfulness. Servanthood
ʿulamā (sing. *ʿalim*): scholars.
ʿulūmu ʾl-awwalīna wa ʾl-ākhirīn: knowledge of the "Firsts"and the "Lasts"refers to the knowledge God

poured into the heart of Prophet Muḥammad during his ascension to the Divine Presence.

ʿulūm al-Islāmī: Islamic religious sciences.

Ummāh: faith community, nation.

ʿUmar ibn al-Khaṭṭāb: an eminent Companion of Prophet Muḥammad and second caliph of Islam.

ʿumra: the minor pilgrimage to Mecca, performed at any time of the year.

ʿUthmān ibn ʿAffān: eminent Companion of the Prophet; his son-in-law and third caliph of Islam, renowned for compiling the Qur'an.

walad: a child.

waladī: my child.

walāyah: proximity or closeness; sainthood.

walī (pl. *awlīyā*): saint, or "he who assists"; guardian; protector.

wasīlah: a means; holy station of Prophet Muḥammad as God's intermediary to grant supplications.

wāw: Arabic letter و

wujūd, al-: existence; "to find,""the act of finding,"as well as "being found."

Yʿaqūb: Jacob; the prophet.

yamīn: the right hand; previously meant "oath."

Yawm al-ʿahdi waʿl-mīthāq: Day of Oath and Covenant, a heavenly event before this Life, when all souls of humanity were present to God, and He took from each the promise to accept His Sovereignty as Lord.

yawm al-qiyāmah: Day of Judgment.

Yūsuf: Joseph; the prophet.

zāwiyah: designated smaller place for worship other than a mosque; also *khāniqah*.

zīyāra: visitation to the grave of a prophet, a prophet's companion or a saint.

Other Publications of Interest

Mawlana Shaykh Nazim Adil al-Haqqani

- The Sufilive Series (2010)
- Breaths from Beyond the Curtain (2010)
- In the Eye of the Needle
- The Healing Power of Sufi Meditation
- The Path to Spiritual Excellence
- In the Mystic Footsteps of Saints, 2 volumes
- Liberating the Soul, 6 volumes

Shaykh Hisham Kabbani

- The Sufilive Series (2010)
- Cyprus Summer Series (2010)
- The Nine-fold Ascent
- Who Are the Guides?
- Illuminations
- Banquet for the Soul
- Symphony of Remembrance
- Healing Power of Sufi Meditation
- In the Shadow of Saints
- Keys to the Divine Kingdom
- The Sufi Science of Self-Realization
- Universe Rising The Approach of Armageddon?
- Pearls and Coral, 2 volumes
- Classical Islam and the Naqshbandi Sufi Tradition
- Naqshbandi Sufi Way
- Encyclopedia of Islamic Doctrine, 7 volumes
- Angels Unveiled
- Encyclopedia of Muḥammad's Women Companions and the Traditions They Related

Hajjah Amina Adil

- Muḥammad: the Messenger of Islam
- The Light of Muḥammad
- Lore of Light / Links of Light
- My Little Lore of Light, 3 volumes

Hajjah Naziha Adil Kabbani

- Secrets of Heavenly Food (2009)
- Heavenly Foods (2001)

Lightning Source UK Ltd.
Milton Keynes UK
UKOW06f1448281217
315194UK00006B/851/P